A Perfectly Imperfect Preemie Mom

Dawn Kim-Romo

Aurora Celadon Publishing LLC

For those who love.

A Perfectly Imperfect Preemie Mom
Dawn Kim-Romo

ISBN: 979-8-218-90585-9

CONTENTS

PART TWO
MY PREEMIE LESSONS

PREFACE

"Come and listen, all you who fear God,
and I will tell you what he did for me."
Psalm 66:16

S even years it took me. Seven years to finally open up about my struggles as a preemie baby's mom. I am a mother of a child born prematurely at thirty-two weeks, and I like to refer to myself as a preemie mom. I think the term preemie mom is easier to say, but in reality, there is nothing really easy about being one.

My original intent in writing was to evoke catharsis for myself. I had been on such a long and emotional journey that I wanted some closure for that part of my life. So, I began to write, and boy did it all come flooding back. The feelings, the memories, the struggles all rose to the surface and engulfed my nights and days with nonstop writing. Though curiously, things were a little different this time. No longer living in the thick of it, it was more like

I was an outsider looking in and delicately recording the past with clear intent and a sense of peace.

At the beginning of my journey, I considered my writing solely for me and entirely as mine. But over time, and as I thought about other parents of preemie babies, I began to think of my writing not just for myself but as something that could help others and, more importantly, as a way to honor God. Preemie babies and preemie parents are born every day, and with each birth comes much heartache. So, to all the preemie moms and dads who are struggling out there, I present my testimony—my humble gift to God—as a symbol of hope. Our preemie struggles are real, but so is the Lord our God. His faithfulness is real, and He can help us overcome anything.

PART ONE

MY PREEMIE BEGINNING

"Jesus looked at them intently and said,
'Humanly speaking, it is impossible.
But with God everything is possible.'"
Matthew 19:26

CHAPTER ONE

Introducing a Preemie Mom

"My health may fail, and my spirit may grow weak,
but God remains the strength of my heart;
he is mine forever."
Psalm 73:26

When my son was born early at thirty-two weeks old, my whole world instantaneously turned upside down and inside out. His premature birth was unexpected and not at all planned for. The doctors could not tell me the exact reason why my son came two months early. In fact, no amount of medical tests, biopsies, or physical exams could unravel his early birth mystery. Medical responses were generally the same: "We can't pinpoint the exact cause of your preterm labor. You had a placental abruption, but did the abruption cause the contractions or did preterm contractions cause the abruption? We do not know, but what we do know is your contractions wouldn't stop."

As a perfectionist, the responses I received brought me absolutely no comfort and sparked bouts of self-criticism and mom guilt. To this day, I still cannot tell you the exact cause of my premature delivery. However, I can say that gnawing, desperate need to know why is no longer with me. God released me of that burden, and I am ever grateful.

As a preemie mom, I experienced a gamut of emotions: love, anxiety, joy, sadness, excitement, fear, contentment, guilt, thankfulness, and regret. My first year as a preemie mom was filled with disquiet about my life's trajectory. On so many occasions, I questioned if God wanted good things for me. My situation became even harder when I chose to deal with things all by myself. While I took excellent care of my son, I stumbled into the nadir of my life. I did not know how to take care of myself physically, emotionally and, most importantly of all, spiritually.

Fortunately, life did get better. After taking a giant leap of faith that God was and would continue to be faithful to me, I started to experience real peace. I went back to church, joined a Bible study class, prayed daily, and participated in a mothers' group. I got out of the house on most days, took my son to weekly playdates with children around his age, and volunteered with my church's children's ministry. Slowly but surely, others started to notice the transformation within me. As I truly began to believe God would redeem my situation, my torrent of negative emotions was replaced with contentment and peace. My anxiety over my son's health eventually became anticipation of the wonderful things to come. In essence, my life changed once I allowed myself to grow in God's timing and love.

CHAPTER TWO

Olé!

"For everything there is a season,
a time for every activity under heaven."
Ecclesiastes 3:1

There was just something about the summer of 2014. I was in the second year of my doctoral program, and I had finally given up my weekend job as a retail pharmacist a few months earlier. I had my Saturdays back! To make things even sweeter, I had been awarded a fabulous and highly competitive doctoral grant that paid a monthly stipend. This allowed me to work from home and at a leisurely pace. Aside from a few weekly meetings with my advisor, my schedule was my own. Mere months before, my life was a hectic rat race dictated by others, but now it was smooth sailing. I had the time and space to focus on just one thing: writing my dissertation. Once that was successfully defended, my career was sure to take off. I was in a good place.

That same summer was the World Cup. Soccer games broadcasting from Brazil were on the television at full blast as I typed my dissertation. I could not help it. To me, soccer was just so much fun. In high school, our team dynamic was amazing. There were a ton of wonderful moments. The camaraderie, the excitement, the cool spring air, lighthearted jokes, and the thrill of scoring a hat trick. Soccer represented a simpler, happier time of my life, and I was glad to be surrounded by the commotion of the Brazilian World Cup.

With its lively music and exciting culture, the World Cup games had begun to strip away the years of stress within me. Stress had done some crazy things to my body, and when it was gone it was like I was a whole different person. It is no wonder I got pregnant so easily.

The morning I found out I was pregnant I awoke with a start. I had experienced one of those rare dreams where I could remember everything in vivid detail. I gently nudged my husband awake to recount every scene. The next thing I knew he was fast asleep again while my feet were hitting the carpet floor with gusto as I raced to the bathroom.

CHAPTER THREE

A Summer's Dream

"Such knowledge is too wonderful for me,
too great for me to understand!"
Psalm 139:6

B efore I knew it, I was searching frantically, headfirst in the bathroom cabinets. After successfully finding the pink rectangular box, I followed its instructions precisely. I sat on the edge of the bathtub and waited patiently as the minutes counted down. I asked myself, "Could it really be true?" My mind wandered back to that dream.

The room was filled with wisps of gray and white smoke. A plethora of incense sticks burned while hovering mid-air. Though thick and warm, the air was surprisingly pleasant. I floated slowly toward an aged and dignified woman seated upon an elevated dais. She was bathed in a soft glow illuminated by gentle lights. Resplendent silk cushions were delicately spread across the floor. In noticing my presence, she shifted ever so slightly in her seat. Gracefully turning her head to gaze at me from the corner of her eye, I saw her stoic yet inviting face. She blinked once before returning her sight back to the table in front of her.

As my body drifted lazily towards her, my mind raced. My heart pounded with excitement as I drew my breath. Without reserve, I suddenly blurted out, "You must be my grandmother!" A slight turn of the chin and a clever smile was her response. Her ancient, steady eyes revealed no answer. She serenely turned her attention back to what was on the table. Believing I would not get a response, I optimistically held on to the certainty we were somehow related.

As my body drifted forward at a snail's pace, the perfume of the burning incense wafted among us. She turned her body fully in my direction and softly whispered, "You're pregnant." Having been stuck on the idea that I was meeting my grandmother for the first time in my life, I heard her words but did not process their meaning. My drifting stopped, and we came face to face. Once again, she uttered, "You're pregnant." With a broad smile, she picked up a plate from her table. On it sat a colorful and unusually-elongated Korean rice cake. She held out the *mujigae-tteok* for me and stated, "It's your pregnancy test. See?" I stared at the long and skinny rice cake with its brilliant colors of pink, yellow, green, and white. The silliness of it all made it very tempting to laugh. But even in my dreams, I did not dare. I pursed my lips and smiled on the outside while chuckling with delight on the inside.

I told myself to look up and take in the scenery. I watched gray smoky wisps swirl into delicate curlicues. From the corner of my eye, I saw white puffs of smoke become fluttering butterflies before dissipating into thin air. I looked again at the old woman. She locked eyes with me one last time before returning her gaze back to her table. With that my presence was no longer needed. My body was quickly pulled backward, and I took it all in one last time. I watched as her silhouette and softly lit room slowly faded into dark nothingness.

Ding! The timer brought me back to reality. I looked at the pregnancy test. One clear pink line and one faint one. My pregnancy dream was right— I was indeed pregnant. In my astonishment, I squealed with excitement. From the bathroom, I could hear the sounds of rustling covers and two separate yet unequal thuds hitting the floor. My dog, who had been sleeping at the foot of our bed, greeted me first. My husband, now fully awake, stumbled in. He looked at me and then at the pregnancy test. "Are you really pregnant?" he asked. I nodded, still in shock. He leaned against the doorframe and scratched his head before whispering, "That's crazy."

CHAPTER FOUR

Sudden Contractions

"A cheerful heart is good medicine,
but a broken spirit saps a person's strength."
Proverbs 17:22

The moment I found out I was pregnant I think our sweet Boston terrier realized it too. Aside from his new habit of enthusiastically sniffing the air in my direction, my dog gradually became more protective of me. He started to sleep on my side of the bed at night, and he would not leave my presence during the day. Throughout my first trimester, my bouts of morning sickness were unrelenting and often lasted the majority of the day. The only relief I could get was through sleep. So, I napped on the couch as my dog cuddled up next to my belly. Whenever I got up, he would follow me around the house with perked ears and concerned eyes. Over time, his usually long walks with my husband became noticeably shorter. No longer interested in lengthy smelling walks, my dog did his business then rushed back home. In the end, I think he wanted to make sure I was always safe.

Our dog was in a strange mood the night my contractions began. I admit I had not been paying much attention to him because I was in a bit of pain. For a few hours, my belly had been cycling through waves of hardening and relaxing. I was in discomfort, and as this was my first pregnancy, I did not know what was happening. My husband paged the on-call nurse, who relayed that I was only experiencing Braxton-Hicks contractions (or false labor pains). At thirty-two weeks along, it was far too early for me to be in labor. We accepted her advice and avoided going to the hospital. The possibility of premature labor never even crossed our minds. Both baby and I were perfectly healthy in every way. We thought we were fine, but our dog knew something was up.

When my husband went to rouse the dog for his last walk of the night, he flat out refused. He would not budge from my side. When my husband attempted to pick him up, he ducked left and then right across the bed to avoid his grasp. After much squirming around, my dog sat next to me again and lay like a heavy sack of potatoes against my belly. I encouraged him to go outside, but instead he got up to scramble away once more. This time, he initiated a low growl directed at my husband. Confused by his behavior I asked, "What in the world is going on?" We could not understand why he was acting so crazy. My dog loved my husband, but in that moment, he was acting a bit hostile. He would not obey. He did not want to leave my

13

presence. Jostling between my body and the edge of the bed, he continued to dodge my husband's swift hands. Having had enough, my husband quickly grabbed his front paws. A split second later, my husband was howling in pain. Our dog had bitten down fast and hard!

While laughing at the scene hilariously playing out before me, I demanded that my husband stop messing around with the dog. Laughing made the pain worse, and all I wanted to do was go to sleep. With the sudden change in my voice, the dog stopped in his tracks. Seeing his chance, my husband grabbed his trunk and rushed him out the front door. Once they returned, I drifted to sleep as my husband grumbled how the dog had refused to walk a single inch and that his hand was now numb with pain.

CHAPTER FIVE

Two Very Long Days

"Then Jesus said, 'Come to me, all of you
who are weary and carry heavy burdens,
and I will give you rest.'"
Matthew 11:28

S leep had evaded me most of the night as the pain continued into the
morning. With the frequency of my contractions increasing to every
seven to twelve minutes, we were sure something was definitely wrong. So,
we called the obstetrician's office as soon as they opened to make a mid-
morning appointment for me.

At the doctor's office, I was led to a small room furnished with a blue
recliner and a tocodynamometer machine to measure my contractions. A
belt was placed snugly around my belly, and I was instructed to rest

comfortably in a semi-reclined position. While rhythmically breathing through the contractions, I sat waiting for the time to quickly pass. Twenty minutes later, a nurse returned to read the tocodynamometer printout. Looking at me skeptically, she declared that no contractions were detected. "How could this be?" I asked. I was in pain. My husband could clearly tell I was in pain too. Something was wrong. I was about to respond further when a strong contraction hit. I immediately hunched over in pain and held my breath. Right on cue, the nurse stepped forward and placed her hand on my belly and pressed down gently. "Oh! You are having a contraction. Yes! I can feel it. It's happening," she said with certainty while slightly jiggling my belly with her hand. She repositioned the tocodynamometer belt—this time over the correct part of my belly—then left the room. Now, my husband and I watched with intention as the machine printed out bell-shaped curves onto pages of graph paper.

Twenty minutes later, the nurse returned to read the updated results. Nodding with satisfaction, she carefully tore the graph paper from the base of the machine and removed the belt from my belly. She led us to another room to meet with the obstetrician. Upon speaking with the obstetrician, we learned the team still believed I was having Braxton-Hicks contractions. Being only thirty-two weeks along, it was far too early for real contractions. Also, I seemed so calm for someone who was truly in labor. Too tired to react, I sat there quietly and dejectedly. I knew I was about to be sent home to deal with the painful contractions all by myself. But before that could happen, I advocated for myself one last time. I requested a pelvic exam, which ended up being one of the most painful things I had ever experienced. But upon its completion, we learned two things: I was two centimeters dilated, and I was in true labor. The obstetrician quickly made arrangements to admit me to the hospital next door.

At the hospital, I learned I was being admitted for preterm labor. The goals were simple. They wanted to stop my contractions with various medications and inject me with two corticosteroid shots twenty-four hours apart to help with the development of my son's lungs. As soon as I was hooked up to the continuously infused magnesium sulfate drips, I became endlessly nauseated. But as the medications started to kick in, my contractions slowed enough to allow rest. Once I was asleep, my husband went home to pack an overnight bag for us and collect our dog to board him at the veterinarian's office.

Twenty-four hours later, I was given the second corticosteroid injection. I felt so proud I had made it thus far. All I had to do was hold on a little longer to allow the second injection to take effect. As the day passed by, I catnapped. To my dismay, the contractions never subsided.

It was the middle of the night when I was awoken by the nurse. She explained that the team recommended I receive an epidural since the contractions were not stopping. After being wheeled to another room, I sleepily perched myself atop the examining table and waited.

The anesthesiologist walked into my room rubbing his eyes and yawning. He also had been roused from sleep, and I felt compelled to apologize for the inconvenience. He waved it off politely saying it was no problem and that he was used to it. Maybe it was due to nerves, but I started to tell him that I was sad my son was going to be born early. He paused momentarily before reaching into his pocket. He pulled out his cell phone and flipped through several screens before showing me a picture of two toddler boys. "This is my second one. He was born early," he said pointedly. I asked him if his son was healthy. With a chuckle he responded, "He's now bigger than his older brother." I looked at the picture again. Feeling relieved, I asked him the one question that was bothering me the most: "Do you know why he came early?" He looked down, further concentrating on opening the medication box in front of him. He shook his head humbly and said, "No."

With gentle and precise hands, the anesthesiologist inserted the needle into my spine. After the epidural was successfully placed, he asked me to test out the pump to make sure it was working. Upon pushing the red button, I felt immediate relief. Feeling grateful for his excellent technique and kind bedside manner, I thanked him before he departed the room.

Upon returning to my hospital room, the nurse asked me if I had slept properly since being admitted. I shook my head. I had not had a decent night's sleep since the night before my contractions began. She left the room and then soon returned with a sleep aid in hand. I swallowed the little tablet with stark cold water, and before I knew it, I was sleeping like a baby.

CHAPTER SIX

Unexpected Assurances

"May your Kingdom come soon.
May your will be done on earth, as it is in heaven."
Matthew 6:10

Gentle streaks of shimmering whites and yellows flashed before me. A voice resounded, "Thy will be done. Thy will be done." I looked around to see where the voice was coming from. "Do not be afraid, my child. Your son is coming. He will be born healthy today," the voice said. I peered with squinted eyes at the silhouette behind the glaring light before me. It was hard to see past the shining rays, akin to peering at the sun in all its radiance. I closed my eyes. Although I could not see His face, I knew it was Him. It was Jesus.

Standing before me was the King of kings and Lord of lords. Yet He stood there patiently, waiting for me to respond. So, I asked, "Will my son be okay?" "Yes, but he will be small," Jesus replied. Without skipping a beat, I further asked, "Will I have enough money to pay for all of this?" Jesus assured me that I would be taken care of, and that to my dying day, I would always have enough. His words were a comfort to my heart.

A moment later, I noticed another being standing nearby. His face I clearly recognized. A tragic death had taken him from us too soon. But now, he was standing before me and staring back peacefully. He smiled softly before turning away. In the blink of an eye, they were both gone.

I awoke to the pain of a very strong and prolonged contraction. While lying in the dimly lit hospital room, I watched the drops of magnesium sulfate drip slowly within the tubing of my intravenous line. As the nausea began to set in again, I turned my head to whisper to my husband who was asleep in the chair next to me. I said, "Are you awake? I just saw Jesus in my dream, and your brother was there too."

CHAPTER SEVEN

Delivery Day

*"You go before me and follow me.
You place your hand of blessing on my head."
Psalm 139:5*

The next morning my contractions were still ongoing. In fact, they had increased in frequency and strength. Despite the potency of the epidural, I began to experience hip discomfort. I repositioned myself in any way I could in order to find some semblance of relief.

By early afternoon, the nurse let me know I was now six centimeters dilated. Despite everyone's best efforts, my contractions were not stopping. My labor was progressing. After receiving a page from my nurse, the attending obstetrician strolled in. She was in a jovial mood. She introduced herself before informing me that today was the day my baby would be born.

The goal was no longer to slow the contractions but to speed them up. The doctor proceeded to further induce labor by breaking my water and administering oxytocin. A few minutes later, a wave of uncontrollable shivering overtook my body. I let out a soft whimper, which caught my doctor's attention. She gave me the once over. "You got the mama shakes," she said playfully before shimmying out my hospital room door.

I was already pretty tired. I had been having contractions for the last three nights, and sleep was fragmented at best. This was my first baby, so I knew there would be more hours of labor to endure. Steadily, my contractions came quicker and lasted longer. By the time I was ten centimeters dilated, my contractions brought on a natural desire to push. The nurse paged the obstetrician again, and by the time the baby was crowning, I had not realized that nine new strangers were now standing in my room. With one last push, my son was freed. Like a champagne bottle uncorked, a surge of bloody amniotic fluid followed right behind him.

CHAPTER EIGHT

The Strong Silent Type

"In the same way, husbands ought to love
their wives as they love their own bodies.
For a man who loves his wife
actually shows love for himself."
Ephesians 5:28

It was the first time in my life that I witnessed my husband on the brink of exhaustion. It had been sixty-five hours of worrying coupled with the lack of sleep. From Sunday evening until the birth of our child on Wednesday afternoon, my husband had made me his priority. Aside from a few saltine crackers found in the hospital break room, he had not eaten. If I was prescribed "nothing by mouth," he too would not eat. If I had to suffer, he wanted to suffer. If I was in pain, he would choose to be in pain as well.

No food, no hot showers, no comfortable bed to sleep in. For reasons I am not sure of, his martyrdom had taken on a whole new level. My husband refused to leave my side except to board the dog and pack an overnight bag.

In seeing my pain and distress, my husband was left feeling helpless. By nature, he was a talented fixer of things, but this was a situation he could not fix. All he could do was wait and see while trying to make my stay in the hospital as comfortable as it could be. In all honesty, he performed his job quite well. Whenever I needed a nurse, he immediately left the room to find one. Being tethered to continuous intravenous drips made my bladder never-endingly full. To help alleviate the pain, my husband periodically adjusted the loops of catheter tubing to allow proper drainage. When the decision was made to further induce labor, my husband never let go of my hand. With joy he watched the birth of our son; with concern he witnessed the bloody fluid that followed. When the obstetrician offered to let him cut the umbilical cord, he calmly brought to her attention that the cord was currently wrapped around our baby's neck. Even without proper rest, my husband remained ever vigilant.

It was my husband who snapped our first baby pictures, and he who resolved to keep watch over our baby as the neonatologist, physician assistant, and nurses took over his care. He walked with the medical team to the neonatal intensive care unit (NICU), staying there until our son was safely handed off. All the while, my dear husband never once complained. For me, he smiled and said reassuring words; for our son, he made sure he was cared for every step of the way.

Once we learned that our baby was able to breathe unassisted on room air and the continuous positive airway pressure machine was no longer needed, it was like we could finally breathe too. *Thank God, the corticosteroids shots worked!* After taking hot showers and eating a full square meal each, my husband and I were temporarily rejuvenated. My once never-ending contractions were finally over, and I could now relax. But the positive energy was only fleeting. Soon, my body instinctively sensed its separation from my baby, and deep below the surface lay a wellspring of emotions that was waiting to burst out.

CHAPTER NINE

Into the NICU

"The Lord is close to the brokenhearted;
he rescues those whose spirits are crushed."
Psalm 34:18

Like me, my husband was experiencing his own internal turmoil. We sat there silently in my hospital room until he finally broke down. The stress of it all had become too unbearable. In his anguish, he confessed his overwhelming guilt. He truly believed he had caused this whole mess. In essence, if he had not gotten me pregnant in the first place, we would have never had to experience our current situation. I would not be in the hospital in pain, and we would not be worrying over the dubious state of our first child. When I heard his confession, I was utterly confused. His words made no sense to me. Clearly, the fault was mine and mine alone. As much as I wanted to comfort him, I could not find any words. Lost in my own torrent of emotions, I shook my head in disagreement as tears fell down my face.

It was now time to visit our son. In a daze, I walked through the halls of the maternity wing toward the NICU. I had not seen my son for several hours, not since I partially held him briefly right after he was born. The events of the last few days happened so fast and in a way so unlike anything I could have ever imagined. My body felt robbed; what remained was a fatigued shell, a broken spirit, and a mind adrift in a sea of confusion. I could not make sense of it all, though I was sure of only one thing: My life was not mine anymore. Everything had gone terribly wrong.

My husband and I approached the set of locked doors leading to the NICU. Surrounded by cameras, we pushed the buzzer on the wall. A voice blared through the adjacent speaker asking, "How can I help you?" My husband replied, "We are here to see our son." As the nurse proceeded to ask for the code on our wristbands I thought to myself, "Is that what we are now, a number?" After being successfully buzzed in, we walked through the final set of locked doors. Immediately, my body went numb. It felt like I had walked into a sterile, halogen-lit institution. For a place that took care of fragile babies, the NICU felt so cold, so uninviting.

Before we entered the main NICU ward, we were instructed to wash our hands. My husband and I stood before two large hospital sinks and read the posted instructions outlining the proper steps to hand washing. We were both healthcare professionals, so aseptic technique was not a new concept to us. In a way, hand washing made complete sense to us, whereas our current situation did not. We squeezed the soapy sponges under the flowing hot water, allowing our emotions to give way to our logical minds. The scent of chlorhexidine danced among the puffs of billowy hot mist coming from the tap. For a moment, the friction of the soapy sponges brought us back to a time that was clear and more carefree. It was easier to focus on scrubbing our arms, wrists, hands, fingers and fingernails than to think about our present situation.

With reddened and raw skin, we entered the main NICU ward. Soft pink drapes hung around individual incubator stations. A cacophony of sounds led us straight to our son. Astonished at the size of his incubator, we noticed that it was easily the largest one in the room. And there he was—our son, all four pounds and five ounces of him—sleeping soundly. He was absolutely beautiful. With great emotion, I stared at him through the incubator's plastic encasement. My husband and I smiled brightly at each other and then back at him. I could feel my heart pounding as if experiencing true joy for the first time in years. We gazed at the lovely sight of our precious, sleeping baby.

CHAPTER TEN

Wires, Wires, Everywhere

"The Lord is my shepherd; I have all that I need."
Psalm 23:1

It was there in the NICU that I finally confirmed with my own eyes that our son was in stable condition. Once he was born, I partially held him for about thirty seconds before he was taken away by his medical team. I had not seen him since, so I was grateful to learn he was no longer in immediate danger.

We stood silently observing our baby in his incubator. He lay amongst a sea of wires. A few were even strategically bundled within the Velcro of his diaper. He had wires connected to electrocardiogram leads and another to a pulse oximeter. He had a nasogastric tube emerging from his nose and an intravenous line inserted in his head. It was an unsettling sight to witness.

I calmly reminded myself that the wires and intravenous lines were necessary for his survival. They were keeping him alive. But it all felt so unnatural, so very wrong. As my relief morphed into pity, my mind flashed back to memories of friends holding their own healthy babies. There were no wires or intravenous lines, just slumbering babies cradled amidst the sounds of their mothers' heartbeats. Conversely, our son lay in a plastic incubator among cold wires and callously beeping machines. He had to survive alone without ready access to warm human touch.

A NICU nurse approached his incubator, snapping me back to reality. She kindly introduced herself before letting us know that our baby was doing well. Looking at me and then at my husband, she asked if either one of us wanted to change his diaper. Realizing neither of us knew how to do this, we politely declined. Ironically enough, our first baby education class was scheduled for the upcoming weekend. There we would have learned the layout of the maternity wing, what to expect during labor, and how to take care of our baby. With our son's early arrival, we had not had the chance to attend the class. We had not yet learned how to change a diaper. Navigating the various tubing and wires through the armholes of the incubator made this task seem that much more daunting. As much as we wanted to change our baby's diaper, we first needed to learn how to perform the task safely.

The nurse acquiesced. While slipping on disposable latex-free gloves, she mentioned that it was probably best for her to demonstrate for new parents how to maneuver the tricky wires and lines. I studied her technique and watched as she delicately rearranged our son's wires and tubing. She laid him atop a clean diaper before unfastening his old one. With one hand, she gingerly lifted both ankles together in one go and then wiped his bottom with her other hand. She neatly removed the soiled diaper before lowering his body onto the clean one underneath. After thoroughly cleansing his belly button with alcohol, she fastened his fresh diaper and repositioned his tubing and wires. She made the process look so easy.

A few hours later, it was time for another diaper change. With newfound confidence, I donned disposable gloves and inserted my hands through the holes of the incubator. I gently rearranged his wires and tubing before carefully changing his diaper. He let out a small cry when the cold wipes touched his skin but became content once his new diaper was fastened. As I sat next to him looking at his small body enveloped in his oversized diaper, I began to experience strong pangs of guilt. I had not been there to help him with a lot of things. I did not change his first diaper, nor was I allowed to hold him during his first nap. I wrestled with the idea that I would continue to let my son down in so many more ways while he lived in the NICU.

CHAPTER ELEVEN

The Gift of Mom's Milk

"Then God opened Hagar's eyes,
and she saw a well full of water.
She quickly filled her water container
and gave the boy a drink."
Genesis 21:19

At my first NICU visit, I learned that my breast milk should have already arrived. Any remaining gratitude I had turned to panic as his neonatologist and nurses emphasized his need for my milk. My son did not have enough time in utero to receive adequate stores of antibodies, calcium, or fats. As a preemie, he needed my natural immunity most of all. While infant formula could be an acceptable alternative, they insisted that "breast was best" for fragile infants.

In wanting to provide the first meal for my son, I returned to my room and pumped in earnest. But in my state of stress nothing arrived. No colostrum, no milk, nothing, nada. I thought of him laying helplessly in his incubator and asked myself, "What kind of mother am I?" I continued to pump every few hours with no success. With guilt, I beat myself up for not being able to help my son during his greatest time of need.

The next morning my milk was still nowhere to be seen, so my son was provided with total parenteral nutrition infused through a vein in his head. Alarmed by the intravenous line attached to my son's scalp, we asked if this type of placement was safe for our baby. The NICU nurse reassured us that it was perfectly fine. With the extra time, I mustered up what little courage I had left and continued to pump every two to three hours around the clock.

The next day, the decision was made to start oral feeds. Time was up, and my milk was needed now. When I arrived at the NICU, I immediately strapped myself to a hospital-grade breast pump. Still without success, I panicked before asking the nurse, "What do I do if I can't make any milk?" With kind eyes and a gentle smile, she reassured me not to worry. If I consented to it, my son could receive donated breast milk until mine arrived.

The following day, my obstetrician visited my room to check on me. In witnessing my depressed state, she admitted that she also experienced immense guilt over not being able to provide milk for her first baby. Though her baby was born full term, her milk never came. My baby, on the other hand, was born two months early. With my mind in a state of shock and my body exhausted from prolonged labor, it was not unreasonable that my milk had not yet arrived. Hearing her words must have been reassuring enough because the first drops of colostrum began to fall while she spoke. Seventy-two hours late, my milk had finally arrived.

CHAPTER TWELVE

Breathe, Just Breathe

"I am worn out from sobbing.
All night I flood my bed with weeping,
drenching it with my tears."
Psalm 6:6

A couple of days later, I was discharged from the hospital. It was early evening, and my husband and I were very tired. Our preemie ordeal had taken its toll on our minds and bodies, and we longed for the comfort of our own home. I personally had not been outside the hospital for over six days, and I was ready to be free from its halogen-lit halls. With a mix of emotions, we said goodbye to our baby in the NICU and drove away from the hospital under an orange setting sun.

On the way home, we made a pit stop at a big-box store. It had a hospital-grade pump available for rent. My personal pump was still en route, and I needed to continue pumping to keep my milk supply up. As we pulled into the parking lot, I thanked my husband for arranging the rental. Having access to an electric breast pump eased my anxiety, as it was one less thing for me to worry about.

Ninety-five dollars later, we were out of the store and walking back to our car. As my husband loaded the bulky machine into the backset, I noticed a couple parked adjacent to us a few rows down. In the front seat of a metallic gray SUV sat a mom with her newborn baby. It was late, but I could see she was physically tired. Her face was painted with exhaustion, and her demeanor was irritable at best. Behind her SUV, a man wrestled a large box out of a shopping cart. I glanced back at the newborn strapped to her chest. The baby was small, but not as small as ours. Perched atop its head was a knitted beanie with stripes of pink, white, and blue. It was the same type of beanie my son wore in the NICU. Strong emotions swelled within me. Before leaving the hospital, I was handed a beanie to take home with me. As I watched her baby, I thought of the neatly folded beanie stored inside my overnight bag.

Unnoticed by the couple, I watched the scene play out before me. The sun had almost set, but her husband continued to struggle with installing the new car seat. I glanced back at the woman. She had an anxious, dejected look on her face. It seemed she and I were both going through our own newborn-related issues. My husband hopped back in the car and paused to

36

watch the couple with me. "It seems like all new parents struggle. That baby looks like a newborn too. It's okay, we shouldn't feel so bad," he urged softly.

When we walked through the front door of our home, we were warmly greeted by our dog. My thoughtful mother-in-law had retrieved him from the veterinarian's office for us that day. He was a sight for sore eyes. Our dog was ecstatic to see us. He jumped up, spun around, and licked our hands and faces. Seeing his unconditional love for us made the tears flow. So much had happened in the last six days, and all our pain and frustration came flooding out. My husband hugged our dog, while our dog sat patiently waiting with concerned eyes.

After showering and then pumping one last time, I readied myself for sleep. I sat on the edge of the bed and gently squeezed the colorful beanie in my right hand. Suddenly and without reason, I placed the beanie on my dog's head. I chuckled softly as he sat there patiently. Obediently, he did not shake the beanie off. I looked away and thought of my lonely son in the NICU. I missed my baby terribly and wanted him home. Teary-eyed, I lay my head on my pillow. When my husband returned from his shower, he held me close as we cried ourselves to sleep.

CHAPTER THIRTEEN

Baby Shower Blues

*"When God's people are in need,
be ready to help them.
Always be eager to practice hospitality."*
Romans 12:13

That first night home was the hardest, but things got a tiny bit easier over time. My baby's stay in the NICU was a mix of medical ups and downs. It seemed he would improve a little before a new health problem would pop up. Two steps forward and one step back. It was an emotional rollercoaster for my husband and me, but we persevered somehow. Having a routine helped. We visited our son daily, so much so that the NICU nurses knew us by name. We also got used to seeing and talking to our baby through his plastic incubator walls. My husband and I took turns bottle-feeding him skin-to-skin since he was only allowed to be held for thirty minutes at a time. He lived most of his life lying on his back in his incubator.

With this whole premature fiasco, my baby shower had been pushed to the back of my mind. However, the event had been on the calendar for months. When I learned I was pregnant, a very good friend offered to host my shower at her house. Having three children of her own, she was a professional at these kinds of celebrations. All she wanted was for me to sit back, relax, and enjoy my shower. Once my baby was born prematurely, my anticipation for this special event morphed into complete dread. I hated the idea of seeing others while being apart from my son. I imagined sympathetic eyes watching me on the outside while thoroughly tearing me apart on the inside. The act of forcing a smile seemed appalling to me. I wondered, "How do I do this?" This was not the happy occasion I had envisioned for myself.

Luckily, one of the shower hostesses anticipated my worries. Several days before the shower, she sent out a thoughtful email to the party attendees requesting that they avoid asking us questions about our NICU baby. She did not want well-meaning friends to inadvertently derail the festivities with uncomfortable questions. She just wanted a happy occasion for mom and dad. She also relayed that our son was healthy but needed to remain in the NICU to grow.

Several days before the shower, we were told mounds of baby gifts were waiting for us. Friends and family had been mailing gifts to the hostesses' houses for several weeks. Even though I wanted to cancel the shower, I could not let anyone else down. I had already let my son down in the biggest way. I did not want to be a failure, a disappointment again. It was my duty; I decided the party must go on.

The day of the shower I got dressed reluctantly, put on a beaded headband, and forced myself out the door. With his head held high, my husband looked at me through dark aviators while squeezing my hand. He smiled. His friends were also planning to attend, and the one who had agreed to be the official photographer was already there. It felt so odd seeing my husband excited to partake in something I very much dreaded. But his joy made me realize one thing: not canceling was the right thing to do.

Walking through the front doors of that beautifully decorated house, filled with green and blue decorations, turned my dread into instant relief. A darling cake shaped like a baby's onesie laid in the middle of the dining room table among diaper towers and an abundance of delicious food. Familiar faces lit the bustling room. Being surrounded by people I had not seen in what felt like ages was rejuvenating. It was a house full of sincere smiles and genuine laughter. Before this, I could not imagine seeing my friends face to face again. But now, my heart was full as loved ones hugged me and others shared they were praying for my family. I did not need to fake happy emotions; my friends lifted my spirits in their own beautiful ways.

Midway through the party, a long-time family friend approached me and asked about my son. (I think she did not get the email in time.) My side of the room went quiet. The hostess who had sent the email shifted in her seat and watched me with concerned eyes, but I took it all in stride. This sweet lady was very dear to me. In fact, I was her daughter's matron of honor a few years back. Surprisingly, I began to talk freely about my son. Other friends came closer to hear about the NICU and the status of our baby's health. I even pulled out my phone to show everyone pictures of him. Many commented on his adorableness, and others debated whether he looked more like mom versus dad. As my phone was passed around and friendly conversations continued, I became more and more at ease. My fears had been unfounded. There was no pity or judgment. Our friends just wanted to show their genuine care and support for us.

By the end of the party, my husband and I learned that the attendees had purchased every single item on our baby shower's wish list. My son received a crib, mattress, car seat, stroller, swing, bath, bottle warmer, bottles, diapers, wipes, baby clothes, and other miscellaneous items. The larger baby items had been carefully assembled by the thoughtful husband of the home we were celebrating in. With so many gifts to haul, our friends helped us truck them home. The baby shower turned out to be a huge blessing for my family and kick-started the healing process for me. I am grateful that the love and generosity of our friends and family were able to shine through the bitter sweetness of that winter afternoon.

CHAPTER FOURTEEN

Baby Is Home

"Always be joyful. Never stop praying."
1 Thessalonians 5:16-17

After twenty-eight long days, our baby was finally given the green light to be discharged. With much delight and a little bit of fear, my husband and I arrived at the hospital to collect our son. We thanked his NICU team, particularly the nurses who had taken such good care of him. Before leaving, I asked the nurses if we should keep the same NICU routine at home. For the past week, our son had been roused every four hours for a diaper change, temperature check, and bottle-feeding. His baths consisted of being held over the sink as warm water fell across his partially toweled body. The two young NICU nurses agreed that it was a good idea to continue his NICU schedule at home.

To be honest, without a whole team of people, it was a bit nerve-wracking to be on such a strict schedule. Every four hours I got up, pumped milk, woke my son, fed him, changed his diaper, checked his temperature, put him back down to sleep, sterilized pump supplies, and then rested for a little while. An hour or so later, the cycle repeated itself. My son always sleepily drank his milk and rarely finished his bottle within an hour. None of us were sleeping. My husband and I were trying our best, but we were lost. We wanted to show our baby we could take care of him just like the NICU did. Separated at birth, we were like strangers to each other. My husband and I wanted our baby to get used to us and for us to get to know him.

At his first well-baby visit, his pediatrician immediately put a stop to all that NICU stuff. She was adamant that he no longer needed to be on a NICU-based schedule. Looking at us both she said, "You are his mom. You are his dad. You're his parents. You know him better than anyone else in the world." She wanted my husband and me to naturally enjoy our baby and not wear ourselves out with unnecessary and unrealistic tasks. He was now healthy and at home. Checking his temperature throughout the day or waking him up for feeds was not warranted. We were needlessly stressing ourselves out, and with more sleepless nights ahead, she wanted us to stay healthy. The only recommendations she kept were for me to continue pumping breast milk and for us to avoid taking him out in public until he was fully vaccinated.

Returning home with a huge weight lifted off of our shoulders, we immediately stopped all NICU-based tasks. Instead, we focused on learning some new skills like how to safely bathe our son in his new bathtub. However, there was one thing that did not change. Ever since baby came home, our dog had become more and more aloof. He sat alone in his corner of the living room, occasionally eyeing the baby with skepticism. Feeling forgotten, he must have wondered why his pets—my husband and I— decided to make our lives more complicated by bringing this new addition into our home.

CHAPTER FIFTEEN

Milestones with a Side of Mom Guilt

*"Even if we feel guilty, God is greater than
our feelings, and he knows everything."*
1 John 3:20

After my son came home from the hospital, my husband and I resumed our graduate studies full-time. I was fortunate to be able to write my dissertation at home, and my husband was glad to restart his experiments in the lab. School became a welcome distraction for both of us, while providing a sense of routine and normalcy. I cared for my son during the day, and my husband devotedly bottle-fed him at night. I can honestly say my husband was an absolute gem of a partner and father.

The unfortunate truths were that my husband carried a lot of guilt about my suffering, while I honestly believed everything was somehow my fault.

My guilt was constant. If I was unable to pump enough milk for the day, I felt guilty. When my baby did not gain weight or if his gastric reflux was especially bad, I had guilt. When his developmental milestones were not achieved on time, I blamed myself. Despite experiencing my own medical emergency, I felt shame in not being able to carry him to term. Once I graduated with my doctoral degree and transitioned to becoming a stay-at-home mom, I felt guilty for desiring a career. I felt horrible I was not earning any income, but the thought of my fragile son getting sick because of daycare was even worse. Seeing my lonely and depressed dog added another layer of sadness to my growing regret. To sum it up, I lived in my own world of never-ending guilt.

As time passed, my son grew up healthy and strong. By the age of two, he was finally on track with his developmental milestones. By age three, people had no idea he was born prematurely since his skills were on par with or surpassed that of his peers. While my son was successfully reaching his age-based milestones, I was busy stumbling through my own spiritual ones. So, for a year and a half after my son was born, I survived in a rather unhealthy way. Fortunately, after I moved to a new city, I finally received the outside support and care I desperately needed. As I began to share my burdens with others, life got so much better.

As a preemie mom, I learned many important lessons about life. These life lessons led to much spiritual growth and resilience, but most importantly, they serve as reminders of God's protection and provision in my life. I am a mom of a preemie baby, which in my humble opinion, is heroic in itself. Though, if I could have any superpower, I would want the ability to travel through time. Then, I could go back to the very beginning and tell my younger self, "Don't worry; one day, it will all be okay."

PART TWO

MY PREEMIE LESSONS

"For God has not given us a spirit of fear and timidity, but of power, love, and self-discipline."
2 Timothy 1:7

CHAPTER SIXTEEN

Hope and a Future

"Children are a gift from the Lord;
they are a reward from him."
Psalm 127:3

I had a very healthy pregnancy. Aside from a few weeks of nausea during my first trimester, my pregnancy went rather smoothly. My checkups were fine, and my labs were within normal range. My baby grew at a normal pace in utero, and my ultrasounds showed proper fetal development. I did not suffer from preeclampsia or gestational diabetes; I was at a healthy weight and age deemed appropriate for a first-time mom. There was no indication that my pregnancy would ultimately turn course into high-risk territory.

One could only imagine my complete and utter shock when my baby arrived early at thirty-two weeks gestation. I wracked my brain trying to remember all the things I had done during the days leading up to his birth. I asked myself and those around me, "Why did my preterm contractions start? Did I inadvertently ingest something harmful? Did I eat spoiled food or get minor food poisoning? Was it due to high stress levels with my dissertation? Did I not sleep well enough? What in the world could have possibly caused this to happen?" Understandably, I was neither expecting nor ready for my son's early arrival. Both baby and mom were in continuous good health; it never crossed our minds that he could be born two months premature. Thoughts of guilt raced through my head as I laid in my hospital bed. Tired and dejected, I asked myself, "How should I have known? Who could have possibly guessed this would happen?"

Psalm 139:16 beautifully states, "You saw me before I was born. Every day of my life was recorded in your book. Every moment was laid out before a single day had passed." Indeed, God knew this would happen because He knows everything about me! While my birth story unfolded in a most shocking way to me, God was not surprised. He knew, with infinite wisdom, that I would one day walk a tortuous path with a preemie baby. I admit, I wrestled with my thoughts for a long time. If God knew this would bring great suffering, why would He allow my baby to be born fragile and premature? As much as I tried to wrap my head around the idea of God's devotion for me, I could not make much sense of it all. I asked myself, "Am I not His child? Does He not love me?" I struggled in understanding God's character until I was reminded of Jeremiah 29:11: "'For I know the plans I have for you,' says the Lord. 'They are plans for good and not for disaster, to give you a future and a hope.'"

As I read and reread that verse, I started to wonder—to ponder deeply. I laid aside my frustration and attempted to entertain a new thought. If God (1) knew me, (2) recorded every day of my life in His book, and (3) wanted to give me hope and a future, then could it be possible that He was allowing me to struggle for my own benefit? It was a tricky concept and something I eventually pushed to the back of my mind. But, life is funny, and the answers to my questions would unexpectedly hit me like a ton of bricks. As the saying goes, "Everything makes sense in retrospect."

I grew up in the church. From an early age, I understood the importance of God's sacrifice and Jesus Christ's death on the cross. I was a perceptive child, loved the stories of the Bible, and marveled at the Holy Trinity's complexity. But as I grew up, I gradually let go of God's hand to let the world take control. That awestruck wonder I had for God began to fade in my mid-teens. By my early twenties, I started to second-guess my relationship with Him, and by my late twenties, I had stepped away from God and the church to focus completely on myself. I began to pursue the "little g" gods of the world—accolades, accomplishments, higher education, social status, and prestigious careers. These idols became the things I lived for, as I drifted further and further away. God was too powerful and too busy—He certainly had better things to do than to worry about me.

A PERFECTLY IMPERFECT PREEMIE MOM

By the summer of 2014, things were going exceptionally well with my graduate studies. I was in my last year of my doctor of philosophy program and the recipient of a competitive national fellowship. Two life goals had already been successfully achieved. And it was a matter of time before I attained my third: a well-respected career. While extremely excited at the prospect of launching into my next phase of life, something still felt amiss. Many of my desires were being fulfilled, yet I felt incredibly lost and alone.

I could not clearly pinpoint the cause of my discomfort at the time. In fact, it would take years of struggling as a stay-at-home mom of a preemie baby for me to finally understand what was happening. My life was not being fulfilled by serving a bunch of worthless idols—this was all meaningless. In truth, my life was made to revolve around God. He was my Source of existence, the Source of everything. I was to love, honor, fear, and obey God. I was important to Him, and His character was that He would not lose me to a desolate life. Proverbs 16:1 asserts, "We can make our own plans, but the Lord gives the right answer." In truth, God loved me so much that He used a precious preemie baby to beautifully wreck my shallow plans and bring me back to the right answer—to a meaningful and satisfying life with Him.

Being the mom of a helpless preemie baby was, at times, extraordinarily hard, but the experience helped me grow spiritually by leaps and bounds. God sounded a wakeup call that only I could hear and, in the process, provided the proof of His love and devotion that I desperately needed. With a preemie baby, God molded and emboldened me with faith and resiliency.

I now have the confidence to survive whatever comes my way. "I know the Lord is always with me. I will not be shaken, for he is right beside me" (Psalm 16:8). Indeed, the Lord bestowed me with hope and a future.

CHAPTER SEVENTEEN

Beautifully Made

*"O Lord, you have examined my heart
and know everything about me."*
Psalm 139:1

To be perfectly honest, giving birth to a premature baby was the hardest thing I ever had to do. It was the first time in my life where I was truly helpless. I was scared. As someone who needed her ducks in a row, I had subscribed to the following beliefs: With perfect planning I was ready, with robust self-sufficiency I did not need assistance, and with reserved strength and nerves of steel I could power through the toughest circumstances. In one fell swoop, my son's preterm delivery showed my "mantras of me" were complete and total fallacies. Never in a million years would it have crossed my mind to plan for a preemie baby. In fact, my birth plans failed to include any procedures for exigent emergencies or other "what if" situations. I learned the hard way that there was no such thing as perfect planning in childbirth (or for anything in life for that matter) and that I was simply not ready. Similarly, my self-sufficiency vanished the moment I was tethered to my hospital bed. Labeled as high risk for falls, I was given no other option but to lie down and let others tend to my and my baby's needs. Lastly, when my reserved strength failed to stop my physical contractions over the course of sixty-five hours, my nerves of steel dissolved to a puddle as I took in the gravity of my son's situation.

In reminiscing on my intro to motherhood, one thing remains strikingly clear to me: I was in pure agony. My son's premature birth was emotionally painful. My mood was labile and would fluctuate on whether my baby was having a good day or a medically bad one. The hardest part of the whole situation was the physical separation. For weeks on end, we had no choice but to leave our son behind in his lonely incubator in the NICU. I felt I had to push down all my emotions, worries, and negative thoughts. I smiled for those around me, showing I was holding it all together as a new mom. In truth, I did not know how to display my vulnerability in front of anyone but my husband during those NICU days.

Fortunately, my struggles in becoming a preemie mom taught me a thing or two about myself and, more importantly, a lot about God. I unequivocally know that my baby served as the primary catalyst in repairing my relationship with God. At a young age, I had developed a keen ability to self-soothe during distressing times, and as I got older, I depended on this skill more and more. But my preemie-related trauma twisted into something beyond my capability to cope with alone, and I was forced to look outside of myself to find relief from another source. The verse 2 Corinthians 1:3 states, "All praise to God, the Father of our Lord Jesus Christ. God is our merciful Father and the source of all comfort." I soon came to the conclusion that, whether I acknowledged Him or not, God was the true source of everything good in my life.

As my merciful God continued to protect and provide for my preemie son in ways I would have never imagined, I finally began to concede to the idea that God's ways and character were beyond my best ability to understand. As someone who always wanted to be right, I had to accept the fact that my comprehension of God was extremely limited. So, I decided to revisit a few verses sent to me by a dear friend. I reread Psalm 139:13-15 which expressively states, "You made all the delicate, inner parts of my body and knit me together in my mother's womb. Thank you for making me so wonderfully complex! Your workmanship is marvelous—how well I know it. You watched me as I was being formed in utter seclusion, as I was woven together in the dark of the womb."

Having returned to the NICU, I gazed at my son through the clear walls of his incubator. Hooked up to seemingly endless tubing and wires, I observed the delicateness of his tiny frame. His sweet chest expanded with each little breath. His small hands twitched ever so slightly with each jolt awake, only to close his eyes again to fight against the tide of sleep. I peered at the monitor next to his incubator. Green numbers on the screen revealed a small, steady heartbeat. My baby was alive. He was surviving. His preemie body had been marvelously, skillfully, and wonderfully made. In a quiet, dark corner of the NICU, I embraced the sight of God's gentle handiwork. With so much education under my belt, I identified science's inability to explain the complexity of life. Only the eternal Creator holds the secrets to this intricate and marvelous formula.

CHAPTER EIGHTEEN

Peace Unyielding

"May the Lord bless you and protect you.
May the Lord smile on you and be gracious to you.
May the Lord show you his favor and
give you his peace."
Numbers 6:24-26

P eace. God's peace. It's enduring, it's extraordinary, and it's satisfying to my soul. His peace exists beyond logic and is covered in mercy and grace. God's peace is phenomenal; to me, there is nothing like it in this world.

The day my son and I were separated from each other was the beginning of the end of my peace. Stress, fear, and anxiety were unyielding. Each morning, I would wake up, get dressed, and rush to the hospital with great apprehension. Above all else, I needed to make sure my son was okay. Once at the NICU, I would longingly peer through the clear incubator walls and patiently wait for permission to hold my son.

Leaving my son behind in the NICU was always the hardest task of the day. Teary-eyed and silent, I made my long treks back home thinking about how my baby was alone and confined to his incubator. I could only imagine how much he longed for my familiar voice, smell, and touch. Unfortunately, my subconscious took over each night. Horrible nightmares ensued, and they were always one and the same. I would find myself standing helplessly by as I watched large structures, such as buildings, parking garages, and cars collapse around my son's crib and bedroom. In my other nightmares, I would frantically call out for help along chaotic streets while running on hot, black pavement. No one ever came to assist, and I would always collapse from exhaustion. Waking up in a panic, I would find myself already crying. It was the worst. It was an awful twenty-eight days waiting for my son to come home from the NICU, as I definitely experienced some sort of post-traumatic stress disorder.

Once my son left the hospital, life began to improve almost instantly. Thankfully, my nightmares vanished overnight. However, the lingering sentiments of fear and anxiety stayed. So, I decided to try to obtain peace the only way I knew how. I focused on my personal goal of becoming the best mom I could possibly be. I propelled my being into every exceptional caregiver task I could think of. I pumped milk every day and kept his baby bottles at the ready. I followed the same feeding schedule from the NICU, so my son never had to cry out for his meals. For hours on end, I diligently and decidedly watched my precious preemie sleep securely in his baby bassinet. While awake, I held him in my arms except during pumping and "tummy time." I continued the routine of regularly checking his temperature for fevers and sequestered him at home to avoid other people's illnesses.

In a way, my husband and I wanted to show our son that we could take care of him better than the NICU did. We readily placed our preemie's health and safety above our own well-being and comfort. I took excellent care of him during the day, and my husband willingly and diligently tended to his needs at night. Our efforts paid off. Our preemie grew into a very happy and healthy baby boy. However, my successful achievements did little to relieve my own anxieties. Because every night, knocking at my door, was a troubled heart, mental fatigue, and physical exhaustion. In all truthfulness, I was quite unsuccessful at creating my own peace.

Even though things were moving in the right direction, I remained enshrouded by a cloud of unease. I could not understand why my efforts were not making me feel better. I was working tirelessly to accomplish my daily tasks, and as a result, my preemie was growing and thriving beyond expectation. Yet, my sense of peace seemed to be slowly regressing and deteriorating.

Fortunately, it was during a Bible study lesson that I finally began to understand the true concept of peace. John 14:27 states, "I am leaving you with a gift—peace of mind and heart. And the peace I give is a gift the world cannot give. So don't be troubled or afraid." Undeniably, peace was not something I was able to create on my own. I could not earn it through personal achievements or conjure it through merit. It was not something I could bestow upon myself or will into being. Peace would never be born from my worldly talents or abilities. It comes from only one source, and all I had to do was have a little faith and ask Jesus Christ for His wonderful peace.

At the start of motherhood, I was inundated with disquieting thoughts about my preemie baby's health, the NICU, evasive mom's milk, work obligations, mounting bills, and mom guilt. When I look back at all the emotional suffering, my heart aches. It did not have to be that way. If I could go back in time and task my younger self with anything, it would be to ask God for peace. "For everyone who asks, receives. Everyone who seeks, finds. And to everyone who knocks, the door will be opened" (Luke 11:10). I believe that God wants peace for all, including preemie moms.

CHAPTER NINETEEN

The Strong Silent Type, Continued

*"Share each other's burdens,
and in this way obey the law of Christ."
Galatians 6:2*

My experiences as a preemie mom have, without a doubt, profoundly impacted my life. I have learned many invaluable lessons, but one thing remains ever so clear and dear to me: We must depend on fellow believers in difficult times. Christian encouragement and prayer have been life-changing for me, and they have made all the difference between joyfully thriving versus merely surviving. In looking back at my life, I firmly believe a strong Christian support system would have greatly eased the suffering from day one, especially for my husband who agonized in silence alone for so long.

Heartbreakingly, my husband held on to the misguided belief that from the beginning our preemie fiasco was all his fault. He truly believed if he had not gotten me pregnant in the first place, I would neither have had to suffer a painful, protracted delivery nor agonize over the sight of our medically-fragile, preemie son. His guilt was so immense, so overwhelming. I did not know how to help him—I was caught up in my own thoughts of confusion and culpability. Separately but concurrently, we were trapped in our own guilt-ridden snares.

If we had to relive it all over again, we would, instead, invite fellow believers in Christ to walk with us every step of the way. As bearers of the Good News, they would remind us that God's sovereignty knows no bounds: "I create the light and make the darkness. I send good times and bad times. I, the Lord, am the one who does these things" (Isaiah 45:7). Our Christian friends would reassure us of God's omnipotence, omniscience, and omnibenevolence, and thus encourage my husband to not take responsibility for the things in God's realm and control. They would continually uplift us with scripture: "Trust in the Lord with all your heart; do not depend on your own understanding. Seek his will in all you do, and he will show you which path to take" (Proverbs 3:5-6). And for moments too hard for our comprehension, friends would echo the sentiments of Paul and Timothy: "So we have not stopped praying for you since we first heard about you. We ask God to give you complete knowledge of his will and to give you spiritual wisdom and understanding" (Colossians 1:9). Our friends would supplicate on our behalf in order for us to receive God's insight and perfect peace.

Furthermore, my husband subscribed to another misguided yet commonly held belief. Once preterm labor commenced, he felt it was his duty to remain composed at all times. In conforming to "the strong guy" stereotype, my husband purposefully held back his true emotions, as well as some much-needed tears. In my opinion, what the Bible does really well is it provides honest insight into the realistic limits of human nature and what God expects from His people. There are many examples of strong men who displayed great vulnerability during times of distress. Job, David, Mordecai, Jeremiah, Daniel, Peter, Paul, etc. showed instances of helplessness and emotional fragility, all the while remaining loved by and precious to God. My wonderful Lord and Savior is no exception: "While Jesus was here on earth, he offered prayers and pleadings, with a loud cry and tears, to the one who could rescue him from death. And God heard his prayers because of his deep reverence for God" (Hebrews 5:7). When pushed to the brink, strong and courageous men cried. In Christian love, all of us are called to help each other and live out the words of Romans 12:15: "Be happy with those who are happy, and weep with those who weep."

Finally, my husband had the overwhelming desire to fix our preemie situation. But in reality, there was little to nothing that he could actually do. Our son's premature arrival was beyond human ability to fix. Although it was extremely hard for him to accept, my husband would eventually come to learn that putting sincere faith and hope in God was the very best thing he could do going forward. As much as he was not used to it, he had to let go and let God do His thing. Colossians 1:17 states, "He existed before anything else, and he holds all creation together."

As my husband's world crumbled around him, fellow believers would have inspired him to hold fast to God's good promises. God would not fail my husband or his family: "God is our refuge and strength, always ready to help in times of trouble" (Psalm 46:1). Fellow believers would have reassured him by pointing out the ways God had blessed him throughout his life. They would also motivate my husband to seek God's will for his life. God's plans are always the very best for us: "Because of our faith, Christ has brought us into this place of undeserved privilege where we now stand, and we confidently and joyfully look forward to sharing God's glory" (Romans 5:2).

I am profoundly thankful to God for giving me my husband. My husband and I have definitely come a long way. I am grateful to God for providing Christian support during the times we failed to ask for it and in the instances we did not know we desperately needed it. I am also extremely thankful to those who prayed for us during one of the most difficult times of our lives. Support from others is a true blessing—it makes this thing called life so much easier to do. "So encourage each other and build each other up, just as you are already doing" (1 Thessalonians 5:11).

CHAPTER TWENTY

Revisiting Mom's Milk

"My eyes are always on the Lord,
for he rescues me from the traps of my enemies."
Psalm 25:15

I want to focus on the topic of control and how the process of losing it affected me. As a premature baby, my newborn's ability to naturally breastfeed was, for all intents and purposes, nonexistent. His reflexes and muscle coordination were still underdeveloped, which in turn, affected his ability to latch, suck, and swallow. So, I made the best decision I could for my son—I vowed to pump as much breast milk as he needed. I believed my breast milk was the best thing for his survival, and it was a selfless way I could contribute to his good care and health. In my haste and naivety, I assumed expressing milk with the help of an electric pump would be a cinch. But, like many times in life, this was easier said than done.

From day one, no milk arrived. None. Nada. Zip. Zilch. Zero. I was at a loss. I seemed to have found myself trapped in a place where I was failing at virtually everything. After days of fruitless pumping, my son's neonatologist let me know he would be discontinuing intravenous nutrition and initiating oral feeds. My baby needed my breast milk pronto! In witnessing my state of panic, a kind NICU nurse notified me of a donor milk program that would temporarily alleviate our problem. The program allowed healthy, prescreened moms to donate their extra breast milk to babies in the NICU. With a sigh of relief, I consented to his participation, and my son received donor milk as his very first oral feeding.

Despite my initial gratitude for donated milk, I noticed my heart harden over the next few days. A storm of frustration and disappointment brewed underneath the surface. A battle had been declared, and I was losing against my own two breasts! For someone who generally succeeded at whatever she did, persistent failure was a hard pill to swallow. Whatever. I decided not to go down without a fight. I became nothing if not persistent, pumping as if my baby's life depended on it. Tethered to my electric and manual breast pumps, I lived a life of disciplined pumping.

In retrospect, I should give myself a lot of grace. My behavior, although somewhat irrational, was in a way entirely understandable. I had been dropped into a very vulnerable situation, and I was steadily losing control over my life. From the very beginning, I had lost control over my own agency. Long before I was admitted, my husband and I had spent so much precious time trying to convince the on-call nurse and obstetrician that something was wrong with my pregnancy. By the time I reached the doctor's office the morning I was admitted, my lower belly had been cycling through regular intervals of tightening and relaxing for over twelve hours. As someone with a high tolerance for pain, I was able to avoid moaning during each contraction; and as a result, many in the obstetrician's office were skeptical that anything was actually wrong with me. Almost a full hour passed before a different nurse repositioned the tocodynamometer device around my belly and contractions were confirmed. After a very painful pelvic exam, the obstetrician declared I was in preterm labor. In seeing my legitimate pain and frustration, the obstetrician apologized before quickly admitting me to the hospital next door.

Unfortunately, being without a prepacked overnight bag meant I was without some much-needed comforts from home. At thirty-two weeks gestation, I was not expecting to go into labor anytime soon. Despite the many medications I was administered, my contractions did not stop. There was nothing more the doctors could do but wait and see. I, myself, could think of no ways to remedy my condition.

When my baby was born, I got to partially hold him for a mere thirty seconds before he was whisked away by his neonatology team. Later on, at my first NICU visit, I learned it was hospital policy to keep preemie babies within their incubators for most of the day and limit their time outside to a maximum of thirty minutes per session. My husband and I were permitted to hold our baby only during oral feedings and once a day for skin-to-skin time. To my great dismay, I accepted the harsh reality that a lonely incubator would be my son's first home since he was a long time away from being discharged safely. Although his NICU stay was warranted, the physical separation was cruel and lasted for four weeks.

Once my son was born, my baby continued to receive excellent care from his medical team. I, on the other hand and despite my requests to my care team, would not be seen by a doctor for at least twenty-four hours after I gave birth. If truth be told, it was my baby's neonatologist who picked up the phone to inform my obstetrician that no one from the practice had checked on me since delivery. Needless to say, my obstetrician rushed over to examine me. Later, she sent a large box of cookies to my hospital room by way of apology. Since I could not obtain precise answers on why I went into preterm labor, my guilt over my son's situation only grew worse.

So when it came time to provide life-saving milk for my son, I was once again without control. It is no wonder I chose to strap myself to my breast pump. My world was quickly collapsing around me, and I was trying my best to grasp at whatever was within my reach. In truth, pumping seemed like the most helpful thing I could do for my son. In fact, I believed it was the only thing I could truly do for him. In retrospect, I had failed to acknowledge God's control over all of life. I had also forgotten about the power of prayer: "And since we know he hears us when we make our requests, we also know that he will give us what we ask for" (1 John 5:15).

The neonatologist team recommended that I pump every three to four hours in order to mimic my son's natural feeding cycle. While some people would callously tease me about being able to get a full night's sleep with my son in the NICU, I was actually experiencing sleep deprivation. I was following a strict sequence of wake, pump, sterilize, and sleep every four hours. I was exhausted. Pumping was not easy for me; it was time-consuming and physically painful at times. To make matters worse, it was noisy and agitating to my senses. The electric breast pump was far from effective at evoking feelings of warmth or bonding. Despite my lengthy pumping sessions, the whole process was too inefficient, and I was never satisfied with the amount of milk I collected.

Really, the biggest downside to using an electric breast pump was all the necessary cleaning and maintenance it required. With my guilt already sky-high, the last thing I wanted to do was to make my son's health worse from spoiled milk. So after each use, I resterilized all reusable pump parts: plastic tubing sets, backflow protectors, valves, connectors, breast shields, and bottles. With all the constant pumping, I had little energy for self-care and almost no time for well-wishers.

One could say my purpose in life became pumping milk for my son. I stuck to my pumping schedule, lived in my pajamas, took fenugreek capsules, inhaled prescription oxytocin nasal spray, and tried to relax as best as I could. Eventually, my milk flowed abundantly. But at what cost? I had refused all visitors, avoided leaving my home (except to visit the NICU), and driven myself into mental and physical exhaustion. Indeed, I had created my own snare.

Why did I do this? In all honesty, I suspect it was my human way of trying to desperately control something within my crumbling world. Both my baby and our time together had been stolen from me, and I was intent on sacrificing myself in any way that was beneficial for my son. The funny thing was, in order to pump milk effectively, I actually needed a decent night's sleep. About two weeks into pumping, I learned (by accidently sleeping in) that sleeping seven hours a night allowed me to pump enough milk for my son for the whole day. By pumping four times a day, I was able to make more milk than when I pumped six to eight times a day. When my baby finally left the NICU and lived with me twenty-four seven, my body naturally created the right amount of milk needed.

Once I finally decided to ask God to release me from my self-imposed snare, I was fully able to embrace the words of Philippians 4:6-7 which state, "Don't worry about anything; instead, pray about everything. Tell God what you need, and thank him for all he has done. Then you will experience God's peace, which exceeds anything we can understand. His peace will guard your hearts and minds as you live in Christ Jesus." Once I relinquished control and handed it over to God, my milk supply boosted to where I was able to donate two whole gallons of breast milk to the same donor bank that provided my son's first meal. God supplied my every need, while I learned how to leave my desire for control at the foot of the cross.

CHAPTER TWENTY-ONE

A Fearless Preemie Mom

*"This is my command—be strong and courageous!
Do not be afraid or discouraged.
For the Lord your God is with you wherever you go."
Joshua 1:9*

"Whatever you do, do not put your son in daycare. Daycares are breeding grounds for disease. Your son's lungs did not have the time to fully develop in utero, which puts him at high risk of catching respiratory disease. Our hospital has already treated so many respiratory cases this season. Avoid large crowds. Do not take him around others if it is not necessary. All visitors need to wash their hands before touching him. In fact, it would be better for him to have no visitors. Your son's immune system is still catching up. For now, keep him at home with just mom and dad. Only take him out for his medical appointments."

Variations of the medical advice above freely flowed from the lips of the doctors and nurses we came into contact with. My son's NICU team was adamant; we were not to take him around others unless medically necessary. Their stance was a result of professional experience, and they were strict about it. No one wanted to see a once healthy preemie baby return to the NICU. As a fellow healthcare provider, their advice rang true. Before anyone had uttered a word of advice, I had already thought of the different ways I would keep my son safe.

The problem with my definition of "safe" was it was always changing and entirely grounded in fear. When my son was discharged from the NICU, I did whatever possible to keep him healthy. I declined visits from well-wishers, good friends, and unvaccinated family members. My husband and I did not take the baby out unless it was for his medical visits. If we needed groceries or other living essentials, we took turns leaving the house to shop solo. At home, we constantly washed our hands, especially before handling our son. Our level of cleanliness became so rigid that, to this day, our skin has yet to recover from its dryness. Heartbreakingly, we even stopped petting the family dog in order to avoid dander, fur, and outside dirt. I continued with my long-standing role of pumping breast milk around the clock. I freely admit our lives revolved around our preemie's well-being. No sacrifice was too great in order to keep him out of the NICU.

Although my self-imposed seclusion and stringent pumping were far from healthy for me, I adjusted to my new way of life. I was resigned to the idea that this was just how things had to be. And when my baby's pediatrician declared him fully vaccinated and ready for the public, I took her advice in stride, noted it, and continued to keep him sequestered at home. After all, my efforts were working. My son was healthy, growing well, and never needed antibiotics or breathing treatments. Outside of the NICU, he had experienced nothing worse than a runny nose. My world was defined by my impossibly high expectations, and when I met them, I gave myself a well-deserved pat on the back. Yet deep down, I knew fear had invaded deep into my psyche, and I was becoming desperate for a better way of life.

The thing about time is it allows for self-reflection and, more importantly, healing. Years later, I can finally admit without judgment that I was controlled by a major fallacy. Yes, my son was kept safe. However, he was not kept safe because of my sole human efforts. My preemie baby was safe because God, through His mercy and grace, kept him safe. Isaiah 46:4 records God's promise to His people: "I will be your God throughout your lifetime—until your hair is white with age. I made you, and I will care for you. I will carry you along and save you." God made my preemie baby, and He created all the ways to keep him safe. God provided my family with access to good medical care and money in the bank to pay for it. As a mom who desired healing, I had to remind myself that I too am a creation of God. He sees my imperfections, yet God chooses to cherish me anyway. He loved us all so much that He sent Jesus Christ, His son, to die on the cross for the world's sins. I hold fast to the following Biblical promise: "Grace, mercy, and peace, which come from God the Father and from Jesus Christ—the Son of the Father—will continue to be with us who live in truth and love" (2 John 1:3).

As a preemie mom, one of the most profound lessons I learned was to always seek God first because God is sovereign over everything and everyone. He protects and saves us from life's vicious snares. I experienced firsthand how ardent prayer actively fought fears and anxieties. When I was afraid, I would pray for wisdom, strength, discernment, and courage. Then, I would confess my fears and ask God for peace and His will to be done. I would also ask Him to meet my every need (known and unknown) and let me in on His plans. By continuously seeking God, I endured life with faith. Having faith was key to growth. It helped me take the focus off of myself and place it back on where it should always remain—on God. In times when faith eludes me, I echo the words found in Mark 9:24: "I do believe, but help me overcome my unbelief!"

As my son reached important milestones, my faith in God further strengthened. My fears subsided, and I became comfortable with taking him out in public. Our bond grew immensely over our newly found freedom. We spent our time visiting playgrounds, museums, and the city zoo. When the weather was nice and breezy, we rode the train in the park or took long walks with the family dog. My son came along for every errand, whether it was to the grocery store, mall, post office, dry cleaners, etc. On the occasion

I was feeling especially adventurous, we would join dad for lunch at the hospital where he worked. My growing boy was perfectly happy to be out with his mom doing whatever, whenever.

Nonetheless, something major was still missing in our lives. In trying to keep our son safe, my husband and I had made the firm decision to avoid daycares. Unfortunately, this included church nurseries. We were in a dilemma. My husband and I wanted to go back to church after being away for so long, but we did not want to do it at the expense of our son's health. So, I began to pray. I prayed every day that God would lead us to the right church for our family. I prayed He would provide a church with a safe and hygienic nursery environment. I prayed for weeks on end, and at long last, God provided me with the information we needed (at an IKEA of all places).

One day, I was passing through an IKEA showroom when a woman unexpectedly placed a business card in my hand. I stared at its colorful design, and realized it was a church business card encouraging people to come and visit. But before I got the chance to ask the woman any questions, she had already vanished into the bustling crowd. I pocketed the card to look it up on the internet later. When I got home that evening, I learned that the church in question had a wonderful children's ministry. God had provided an answer to my prayers, and it was now our turn to act. After a few months of hemming and hawing, my husband and I finally took a giant leap of faith and walked into that church. As the saying goes, the rest is history!

A PERFECTLY IMPERFECT PREEMIE MOM

I admit it was hard to leave our son with strangers at first, but I am so glad we finally chose to put our trust in God instead. That church, the one I learned about inconspicuously at IKEA, turned out to be the perfect environment for my son. It became the place where I developed priceless friendships, many of which I continue to maintain to this day.

I want to fast forward to the year 2020. Our family (along with much of the world) found ourselves in the midst of a lockdown due to the SARS-CoV-2 virus, and I was experiencing a stark sense of déjà vu. Our family was, once again, sequestering from the public in order to stay safe and healthy. Like many others, we allowed no visitors and avoided venturing out in public unless necessary. Careful attention to cleanliness was our new normal once again. We washed our hands frequently and equipped ourselves with face masks and hand sanitizer. While we took the necessary precautions, I can honestly say that things were very different for me this time around. Previously I sequestered in fear with a preemie baby, but now I sequestered in peace while the rest of the world seemed to be caught up in the chaos. While I had little faith before, overcoming the trials I faced as a preemie mom built within me confident proof of God's care and devotion. God had already delivered my family through our first sequestration, and I knew He would do it again with the pandemic.

Donning my homemade mask and with my bottle of hand sanitizer, I easily ventured out of the house solo. With trust in God and my mind at peace, I happily stood in line for hours, six feet apart from others, and waited for my turn to buy groceries and other basic essentials. With joy in my heart,

I shopped the fabric stores for supplies needed to sew masks for adults and children. I quietly whispered prayers of thanks to God while out in public. I praised Him for His blessing for my family and the opportunity to serve others. I praised God for my husband's job and my family's good health. I watched Sunday church services online with a grateful heart and met with my Bible study group online. I thrived instead of just survived, while relishing God's goodness. I felt invigorated with courage at a time where much of the world felt overwhelmed with fear. For me, there was no fear, only faith. It was the first time in my life where I truly lived out the words of Hebrews 11:6: "And it is impossible to please God without faith. Anyone who wants to come to him must believe that God exists and that he rewards those who sincerely seek Him."

CHAPTER TWENTY-TWO

The Lord Provides, and Then Some

"So don't worry about tomorrow,
for tomorrow will bring its own worries.
Today's trouble is enough for today."
Matthew 6:34

O nce married, my husband and I solidified into a highly driven, career-focused couple. Our personal and professional desires took center stage, and as a result, we pursued advanced graduate degrees and worked very long hours. Most days of the week we saw very little of each other, like two ships passing in the night. In graduate school, our professional and educational desires led us down long, winding, and highly individualized career paths, and because of this, we made some very significant sacrifices in our marriage. Like the plague, we avoided succumbing to life-altering events, such as having children, purchasing a home, and putting down roots. We focused on our studies, while deferring student loan debt. We believed our careers were the ticket to our dreams come true. All we needed to do was stick to the plan and stay the course; everything would eventually fall into place. But once we became pregnant and then had a premature baby, our life plans began to unravel most frighteningly and irrevocably. "We can make our plans, but the Lord determines our steps" (Proverbs 16:9). Indeed, my husband and I were about to experience firsthand how God was going to alter the next steps of our lives.

While I knew becoming a new mom would cause some temporary changes, I did not realize that becoming a preemie mom would require drastic life alterations. No longer could I, in good conscience, place my desires before my own baby's needs. Our son spent his first twenty-eight days of life physically separated from us in the NICU, and this left us emotionally teetering on a delicate balance. My husband had one more year of studies left to go, and he worked very long hours. So, I did what I thought was the best for my whole family—I quickly wrapped up my doctoral studies and quietly graduated with my doctor of philosophy degree. With great sadness, I placed my career plans on hold, turned down two exciting job offers, and accepted my fate as a stay-at-home mom. This decision was not easy—I had dreamed of becoming a career woman for so long. My husband worked in a lab and needed to be physically present to conduct his experiments, and I could not move across the country for a new job. This seemed even more impossible to do with a medically fragile baby in tow. With no one else available to provide individualized, affordable care for my son, becoming a stay-at-home mom became the only path I could reasonably take.

With me no longer in the workforce, a new problem reared its ugly head. My husband and I had always been a two-income family, and I was beginning to worry we were not going to make it financially. Suffice it to say, we could not. We could not survive on one person's graduate assistant salary. Within a few months, money got tight, and we could not afford our basic needs. To make matters worse, the medical bills started to pile up daily. We owed money for our hospital stays, medical procedures, physician visits, specialist care, lab tests, etc. We were inundated with medical debt. With no one to spot us financially, my husband and I found ourselves in new states of worry and panic. We bickered and blamed, threw emotional daggers, and accused each other of selfishness or fiscal irresponsibility. All our arguing was mentally exhausting—it was no way to live. This still remains a poignant time in my life where I wish we offered each other more grace: "Make allowance for each other's faults, and forgive anyone who offends you. Remember, the Lord forgave you, so you must forgive others" (Colossians 3:13).

Generously, God had been working behind the scenes to provide for us. While my husband and I were surprised at the situation we were in, God was not. My heavenly Father knew that one day we would have a preemie baby, so He made sure we had access to excellent health insurance and money for emergencies. Once we paid off our deductibles, we learned our insurance company would cover the remaining medical bills. To say it was a lot of money would be an understatement. Additionally, God had bestowed us with very kind and compassionate bosses, who provided my husband and me with extra paid days off to be with our son in the NICU. Their acts of Christian generosity remain touching examples to me of what it means to be the hands and feet of Jesus Christ. For others who witnessed their generosity, they were the personification of what our loving God can do for His children.

Acutely aware of our needs, God eventually provided a new career opportunity for my husband. Within weeks of submitting his application, my husband was offered a well-paying position in a nearby city. His employer needed him to start within a couple of months, so my husband had to find a way to finish up his studies quickly. However, completing his dissertation within eight weeks was not realistically going to happen. It was only through the grace of God that he was able to negotiate an arrangement with his doctoral advisor. He was given the green light to leave mid-semester, work remotely, and then return to defend his dissertation at a later date. Departing university sans degree was not an easy thing to do. My husband had dedicated so much blood, sweat, and tears to the lab and secretly feared all his efforts could soon go to waste. On the other hand, he was determined to take care of his family, and in seeing his devotion, a fire was lit within me. If my husband was going to make a huge sacrifice for us, then I needed to do whatever I could to prove we were a team. In a new city, my husband worked during the day and wrote his dissertation in the evenings. I dedicated myself to keeping our preemie baby safe, while diligently managing our finances.

In essence, I spurred us on to become very thrifty budgeters. We prioritized God first, our basic needs second, our savings third, and our student loans fourth. From a young age, I was taught that God should always come first. In showing Him my dedication, I dutifully gave for years the first portion of my earnings every paycheck. For the Bible says, "One-tenth of the produce of the land, whether grain from the fields or fruit from the trees, belongs to the Lord and must be set apart to him as holy" (Leviticus 27:30). My husband and I were in the habit of tithing ten percent since getting married, so we continued to do so in the hopes God would continue to bless us as good stewards of His money.

Next, I paid strict attention to all of the money coming in and going out of the house. Using a free monthly calendar found online, I began the painstaking habit of manually recording every dollar spent each day. I documented all expenses (big and small), such as rent, water, gas, electricity, phone and internet services, grocery bills, car fuel and maintenance, medications, and other miscellaneous items. The calendar method was super useful because it kept me abreast of all our daily expenditures and allowed me to easily incorporate new cost-saving plans throughout the month.

Unsurprisingly, the cost of food had become one of our biggest expenses. My husband and I loved to dine out; it had become our favorite pastime. But now as a single-income family, we had to make necessary changes. All restaurant dining had to stop, and eating home-cooked meals became a top priority. At the beginning of each week, I scanned online grocery store saver ads to identify the best deals on fruits, vegetables, meats, and dairy products. I did my best to plan and create inexpensive, well-balanced meals. I almost always prioritized buying the weekly in-house grocery deals over non-sale items and utilized manufacturer coupons whenever possible. I prepared a lunch for my husband to take to work each day, and if we needed to be out of the house around mealtime, I would pack a homemade meal to take with us. While my husband and I sorely missed dining out, we noticed improvements in both our savings and our waistlines.

Likewise, we maintained a practically nonexistent budget for entertainment. I searched for all the free events offered in the area. Our weeks were filled with free family outings to the Children's Museum, the Natural Science Museum, the Museum of Fine Arts, outdoor plays, the zoo, the arboretum, and random festivals. If we wanted to be out of the house for the whole day, we would visit a nearby beach (the parking pass cost ten dollars a year), parks, or nature trails. Unluckily, we did not have date nights since that involved paying for a babysitter, so we just rolled with it. We took our son wherever we went and spent time as a family. Vacations were deferred to a time far, far into the distant future.

Most significantly, my husband and I agreed to sacrifice our day-to-day comfort for heavily reduced living expenses. So, we rented a small apartment, sold our second car, and lived in the inner city within a ten-minute walking distance to work. These specific sacrifices allowed us to save a substantial amount of money on rent, insurance premiums, parking fees, car maintenance, and gas. Pretty quickly, we rebuilt our emergency savings and were able to tackle our biggest financial burden to date: student loan debt.

Even though my husband and I had been in college for over a decade each, our student loans had resulted from our first degrees and were now compounded by tens of thousands of dollars in interest. Our lives were being crushed by financial debt. I can personally attest to the truth of Proverbs 22:7, "Just as the rich rule the poor, so the borrower is servant to the lender." With hundreds of thousands of dollars owed, my husband and I were limited in what types of jobs we could take, where we could live, and how we could spend our money.

In order to be freed from our financial bondage, we made the decision to aggressively knock out our student loans no matter how long it took. Our commitment was solid—we lived like paupers and paid loans like princes. It was not easy. It took a lot of commitment, perseverance, prayer, and an endless amount of grace for ourselves. We lived through six years of austerity, but the great news is God answered our prayers! He released us from our monetary chains when we successfully paid off over $200,000 dollars in student loan debt! It was all so difficult, yet so rewarding. Our financial triumphs proved that, without a doubt, God's devotion to our well-being was genuinely real.

I was once asked, "Why do you tithe so much? Would it be better to put all that money towards your student loans?" The questions were asked rather innocently, so I responded with a rather simple answer. I professed that every good thing in my life came from God. James 1:17 states, "Whatever is good and perfect is a gift coming down to us from God our Father, who created all the lights in the heavens. He never changes or casts a shifting shadow." My family and I lived in a safe home, ate delicious food, had emergency savings in the bank, accessed medical care whenever needed, and remained a loving family. My God was, and continues to be, amazingly generous. He blessed us freely and openly, while we did nothing to deserve His favor. So, if God asks for my "first fruits," I will obey. I would not withhold from God the things He deserves but, instead, will put Him first and hold fast to the promise that He will take care of our every need.

When reminiscing on this time, I am also reminded of Proverbs 16:33, "We may throw the dice, but the Lord determines how they fall." While this sounds slightly ominous at first, it is actually for the best. God is omnipotent, omniscient, omnipresent, and wonderfully omnibenevolent. His ways are the best ways. For me, I am glad that God's plans prevailed over my own plans. Our financial odyssey intertwined with having a preemie baby which, in a way, heightened the desperation of our trials. Our experiences remain profoundly ingrained in our minds and have made us fiscally wiser, more content, and ever grateful for the things we already have.

Now, I truly understand Paul's words in Philippians 4:19: "And this same God who takes care of me will supply all your needs from his glorious riches, which have been given to us in Christ Jesus."

CHAPTER TWENTY-THREE

An Identity Redefined

*"For the world offers only a craving for physical
pleasure, a craving for everything we see,
and pride in our achievements and possessions.
These are not from the Father,
but are from this world."*
1 John 2:16

A wise mom once told me, "You have to take time to mourn your hometown." When I heard those words, I found myself sitting at a Mothers of Preschoolers (MOPS) table in a brand-new city. Her advice rang true. Hundreds of miles away from family, friends, and old stomping grounds, I felt like a stranger in a strange land. Gone were the days of dining at my favorite restaurants or hiking beautiful city trails. I had said goodbye to a city I had loved and lived in for over thirty years. I admit, I was silently grieving. Tragically, my grief was further compounded by another unfortunate feeling: FOMO. FOMO stands for the "fear of missing out," and since becoming a stay-at-home mom, I suffered from major FOMO. My FOMO was ruthlessly and relentlessly stealing my joy. Each day my degree of FOMO seemed to worsen, as career opportunities quickly and steadily slipped between my fingertips.

As a highly educated woman and new preemie mom, I was at a loss of what to do with my life. Lost physically in a new city, and lost emotionally without a support system, I sank deep into my self-pity and frustration. My identity was something I had worked so hard to create, and it was slowly unraveling before my very eyes. For over a decade, my self-worth had been defined and uplifted by my personal achievements and advanced education. By my early thirties, I had earned three degrees (two of which were at the doctoral level). I had invaluable experience as a healthcare provider, interned for a successful consulting firm in Washington, D.C., and earned a nationally competitive pre-doctoral fellowship. I was well on my way to starting a new and exciting career. Once we welcomed a preemie baby into our family, my professional dreams were reluctantly deferred.

People say life is funny. Others say life is cruel. I say life is great at bringing me back down to earth. For many years and for many reasons (some of which I am still coming to terms with), I had wrapped my identity around my personal achievements. If I was doing well, life was great. If I was doing poorly, my self-esteem would nosedive, albeit momentarily until my next achievement came along. My past setbacks always seemed temporary, but this—becoming a preemie mom—seemed more like a long-term failure.

In choosing to place my son's needs over my own desires, I knew nothing else but to set my gaze back on God. In all honesty, I was not happy about it; waiting on God's plans for my life was not an easy thing to do. I had fought for so long with so much inner turmoil, frustration, and disappointment that I had no clue where to start. Although I cannot pinpoint the exact date, I know I eventually got there. With God-given clarity and abundant grace, I embraced the hard truth. My identity was neither something I could create nor fashion from worldly achievements or earthly treasures. No, my identity was lovingly preordained by God and established long before my time: "For we are God's masterpiece. He has created us anew in Christ Jesus, so we can do the good things he planned for us long ago" (Ephesians 2:10).

In reevaluating my life and its new trajectory, I came to see the error of my ways. I realized I had, slowly but surely, allowed the "little g" gods of the world to become the most important aspects of my life. Although never outwardly praising money, prestige, or acclaim, my idols were the things I thought about each morning and at night before bed. My idols, my gods, had become furtively ingrained within my psyche. They subconsciously drove my major decisions, as well as became the things I strove to achieve in life.

Money, prestige, and acclaim are not inherently evil things, but they should never become gods. Scripture is wise in stating, "Guard your heart above all else, for it determines the course of your life" (Proverbs 4:23). Those "little g" gods are deceiving; there is only one true God that exists, and nothing should ever come before Him. Exodus 20:3 records God's explicit command: "You must not have any other god but me." The Apostle Paul's words echo this in 1 Corinthians 8:6: "There is one God, the Father, by whom all things were created, and for whom we live." No gods or idols should ever steal the love, adoration, and devotion meant for God.

My sentiments as a preemie mom began with frustration and apprehension but ended in awestruck gratitude. God had been faithful to me. In times of major FOMO, I deemed myself forgotten by Him, but in reality, it was the opposite. God was keeping me safe. He was breaking me away from a life of worldly disappointment. By removing the distractions, He kept me from repeating history: "They worshiped their idols, which led to their downfall" (Psalm 106:36).

When I finally submitted to the will of God by putting Him first, I saw His good promises come to fruition. God required a change of heart within me before bestowing new career opportunities. My identity needed to be reset and remade. Having lived through the fires, I endeavor to live out the words of Lamentations 3:24: "I say to myself, 'The Lord is my inheritance; therefore, I will hope in him!'"

CHAPTER TWENTY-FOUR

Her Helping Hand

"Give, and you will receive.
Your gift will return to you in full—pressed down,
shaken together to make room for more,
running over, and poured into your lap.
The amount you give will determine
the amount you get back."
Luke 6:38

By the time my son was three and a half years old, I noticed a substantial change within myself. In general, life had become considerably easy for me. Whether it was for Bible studies, MOPS meetings, play dates, or the usual errands, my son and I excitedly ventured out of the house every day. I was having fun, and I relished my new state of being. However, thoughts still nagged at the back of my mind. I could not shake them, so I began to ruminate on my life. I wanted to pinpoint the changes within me. Undeniably, I had walked through some intense fires as a preemie mom, yet in the end, I made it out seemingly in one piece. It was obvious that God had been faithful to me, but what exactly did He do? How had He changed me?

I was encouraged when I read the Book of Romans because, there in those pages, I found my answers. I believe Romans 5:3-5 sums it up quite nicely: "We can rejoice too, when we run into problems and trials, for we know that they help us develop endurance. And endurance develops strength of character, and character strengthens our confident hope of salvation. And this hope will not lead to disappointment. For we know how dearly God loves us, because He has given us the Holy Spirit to fill our hearts with His love." The words of the Apostle Paul rang true in my life. God had affected me deeply through suffering, and as a result, bestowed upon me some new found treasures in life. As a once broken preemie mom, I now lived my life with endurance, character, hope, and joy. Understanding this, I did not want to keep these newfound riches to myself. I desired to be a positive influence for God's kingdom because His impact on my life was so wonderful. In determining the best way I could do this, I decided to focus on supporting struggling moms.

My first opportunity to help other moms in a broader capacity was through MOPS. As a table leader for my MOPS chapter, I had the privilege of serving as a listening ear, a prayer warrior, and an encouraging confidant. My goal was simple—I wanted to make MOPS a welcoming haven for the moms under my care. So, I did my best. I uplifted the moms in my group by cooking meals, hosting get-togethers, scheduling playdates, praying, and checking in via phone or text. I encouraged my table's moms in any way I could. As a mom myself, I knew what it was like to constantly put the needs of others before my very own. I wanted them to feel somewhat pampered and taken care of.

Similarly, my primary reason for serving as a preschool teacher at my local Community Bible Study (CBS) chapter was to assist other moms. I watched over their preschoolers, so they could rejuvenate through Christian fellowship or one-on-one time with God. It was a dutiful decision to make. In the past, I had been a struggling mom and a grateful recipient of others' blessings of service, so I felt it honorable to help the next generation of moms within my community.

Giving back to others has become a very necessary part of my life. As a follower of Christ, I am called to assist others who are struggling. Hebrews 13:16 states, "And don't forget to do good and to share with those in need. These are the sacrifices that please God." Helping others is so important, and I posit this based on the numerous Bible verses and stories on this topic. Our kindness and service to others is absolutely acknowledged by our Heavenly Father. It also allows believers and non-believers to see God's goodness through His people. "In the same way, let your good deeds shine out for all to see, so that everyone will praise your heavenly Father" (Matthew 5:16).

Surprisingly, I found that helping other moms played a huge part in my healing process as a preemie mom. I was astonished! I completely expected to receive nothing in return for my time and efforts, but in reality, serving others helped me find peace with my own circumstances. Although there were no moms under my care with preemie babies, each mom was fighting her own unique battle in life. Whether it was related to surviving a difficult childbirth, dealing with health problems, worrying over a child's growth and development, maintaining a healthy marriage, navigating family dynamics, living on limited finances, etc., I was not alone. My interactions with seemingly ordinary moms showed me that, in a sense, we were all cut from the same cloth. Indeed, motherhood is tough!

In the end, in helping other moms, I helped myself. Not only did I experience camaraderie and gain strong friendships, I learned I was not alone in life. Through the grace of God, I hope to continue to serve others throughout my lifetime, and in turn, live a life full of endurance, strength of character, confident hope of salvation, and love.

CHAPTER TWENTY-FIVE

Our Hill of Life

"Your righteousness is like the mighty mountains,
your justice like the ocean depths.
You care for people and animals alike, O Lord."
Psalm 36:6

M any, many years ago, my husband and I unknowingly walked into the den of a backyard breeder to meet our dog for the first time. Covered in filth and rife with fleas, he was in a weakened state due to poor nutrition and an overwhelming amount of intestinal parasites. His situation was horribly wretched. Much of his life had been spent sitting in a small, dirty kennel—its doorway blocked by a sheet of old newspaper. When I think back on that day, I remember the truth in Proverbs 12:10: "The godly care for their animals, but the wicked are always cruel." My husband and I hated the idea of supporting such a business, but my good friend, who was along for the ride, had already decided to report the breeder for inhumane conditions. So, we agreed to not leave him behind and to give him a life full of love and care.

The thing I loved most about our pup was how expressive he was for an animal. Our beloved dog could articulate his emotions unlike any pet I had previously come into contact with. Like many dogs, he communicated with his eyes. Dark, piercing, and laced with devoted concern, his eyes could easily sway our hearts with the simple lift of the inner eyebrows. I have been told this physical trait uniformly distinguishes dogs from wolves; but whatever the case, its effect was undeniable. With bright eyes, a tilted head, and an inquisitive stare, my husband and I were often left with no other option but to acquiesce to his requests.

Our sweet puppy soon embraced the role of the quiet, emotive actor. This was especially apparent in times where he felt particularly slighted. To this day, I can still recall one particular Thanksgiving when my husband and I accidently forgot to feed him during our haste to prepare our own meal. We had been so busy that we, ourselves, had not yet had our first bite of the day. By the time we sat down late in the afternoon, our dog was nowhere to be found. With much ado, our search ended when we spotted him in another room. Our dog was sulkily sitting upright, half-way facing the corner of the room. Though I know he heard us approach, he continued to keep his head down, eyes closed, and ears pinned back to where they touched. For a Boston terrier, the look was quite impressive. Our dog was so upset with our carelessness that he could not even look up at us. Upon taking in the scene, my husband and I looked at one another before howling with amusement. We could have died from laughter! Our pup had us thoroughly wrapped around his little paw, but we could not have cared less. We loved him. He was our first dog and, in a way, our very first "baby."

Long before the arrival of our human baby, my energetic dog and I spent our free time out in nature. The lake was not far from our home, so we frequently took advantage of its calm, lazy waters. I loved to observe my dog as he peered into the blue depths in search of turtles, fish, and other freshwater life. At the time, my best friend had several dogs of her own, and along with her brood, we would make a day of it. Swimming through cool waters and soaking up the sun, my pup was a water dog through and through.

When the leaves began to change color in the cooler months, my dog and I explored the natural, picturesque trails located throughout the city. There was one specific, rocky hill we would run down as fast as we could only to hike back up again for the sake of exercise. On days after heavy rains, my dog and I would gingerly hop over fallen tree trunks and muddy puddles while exploring the area's cliffs. Life was easy.

It pains me to say that our dog is no longer with us. He died the year the pandemic hit. My husband and I think of him quite often, but our emotions are bittersweet. While precious memories make us laugh and smile, they also make us cry. Not unlike other new parents, our priorities and attention shifted when our son was born. Our evolving family dynamics with a preemie addition made it to where things were never the same for him. Indeed, they were never the same for any of us. It is these thoughts that make my husband and me so sad. The idea of our beloved fur baby feeling neglected leads to overwhelming guilt and regret. But soon after, I pause to catch myself. I make myself remember our dog's true nature. In every memory I have of him, he always prioritized making sure we were okay. So, I focus on the facts: My dog never held grudges, and he always forgave no matter what.

The ashes of our late dog currently sit on a shelf in our living room, and his commissioned painting hangs prominently in the house. From time to time, I gaze at this painting and thank God for giving him to us. Memories of him remind me of Revelation 4:11: "You are worthy, O Lord our God, to receive glory and honor and power. For you created all things, and they exist because you created what you pleased."

To my God in heaven, thank you. To my departed pet, please rest in peace. Till my dying day, I will always cherish you. I miss you dearly, but I remind myself not to be so sad. Because after all, we will always have our hill of life.

CHAPTER TWENTY-SIX

On Solid Ground

"Give thanks to the Lord, for he is good!
His faithful love endures forever."
Psalm 118:1

My preemie baby has definitely come a long way. Every so often, I think back on his four-week-long stay in the NICU. In my absence, I perceived him to be lonely, scared, and confused. The warmth of my womb was suddenly swapped with cold room air, my steady heartbeat replaced by cacophonous noise from the very machines keeping him alive. My son was so small that even preemie baby clothes were oversized for his tiny frame. The NICU invoked bittersweet emotions. I was happy my son was alive and cared for by skilled professionals but, at the same time, sad he was not able to come home with us. Those days were without a doubt the hardest for me.

How I wish I could go back in time! Then, I could share the secrets of survival with my younger self in the hopes of easing my internal struggles from the very beginning. My advice would be simple. First, seek the support of other believers in Christ. Although I had strayed from the church, I still kept in contact with good friends who were strong Christians. I would encourage my younger self to reach out to these friends and ask them to pray with me. The power of prayer is very real! It can uplift emotions, give peace, and embolden hope. The Christian community is there to pray for anyone and everyone, and they can pray in times when our own words seem to escape us.

Second, engage in quiet time each morning for the purposes of praying, reading the Bible, and meditating on God's goodness. I would encourage my younger self to start with the Book of John, which is my favorite book of the Bible. To this day, John's gospel remains a source of comfort and enlightenment for me as it paints a clear picture of who Jesus Christ is in relation to the past, present, and future. I love the descriptions of Jesus Christ as the Word found in the verses of John 1:1-5: "In the beginning the Word already existed. The Word was with God, and the Word was God. He existed in the beginning with God. God created everything through him, and nothing was created except through him. The Word gave life to everything that was created, and his life brought light to everyone. The light shines in the darkness, and the darkness can never extinguish it."

Third, join a support group that focuses on motherhood. I found MOPS International (now known as MomCo) to be a wonderful and timely source of support. It was there that I met more experienced moms who had previously walked in similar shoes and cried the same tears as me. Also, I befriended moms who were in the same strata of life as me and besieged with their own mom-related trials. MOPS was a place where moms came together to encourage each other along life's arduous journeys. I am so grateful for the ladies I met through MOPS, and because of MOPS, I hold the strong conviction that God did not want me to struggle alone.

Fourth, take part in an established, year-long Bible study. Although there are many well-known Bible study organizations out there, I would personally recommend Community Bible Study (CBS). For me, studying the Bible at CBS not only involved learning new facts about God and the Bible, it served as a much-needed catalyst for life change. Walking hand-in-hand with God required me to surrender my old way of life to Him. I had to engage in effectively releasing my need for control by actively placing my trust in God through prayer, petition, and thanksgiving. The continual study of Scripture helps me acutely understand God's will for my life. His instructions are essential for a prosperous and healthy life: "The commandments of the Lord are right, bringing joy to the heart. The commands of the Lord are clear, giving insight for living" (Psalm 19:8).

Fifth, always be grateful for the blessings in your life. The Bible says, "Be thankful in all circumstances, for this is God's will for you who belong to Christ Jesus" (1 Thessalonians 5:18). I could not stress this concept enough to my younger self. The ability to show genuine thankfulness to God, regardless of life's circumstances, is a true gift. It is an intentional action that requires much practice. Praise God for the big blessings He has bestowed, as well as the small ones. Thank Him for all our creature comforts and the things often taken for granted like clean water to drink, fresh air to breathe, air conditioning, and heating. I know God is good and supplies my every need. A big secret to surviving and then thriving is to be grateful for the things we already have.

Alas! I cannot go back in time or mentor my younger self. As much as I wish, I cannot change the past. I can only live in the here and now. And at present, there exist moms of preemie babies who are experiencing the same troubles I once endured. Proverbs 3:27 commands, "Do not withhold good from those who deserve it when it's in your power to help them." So, it is my sincere wish that my testimony be a genuine source of encouragement during trying times. Whether a preemie mom, a preemie dad, an anxious grandparent, or a concerned friend, I embolden you to seek God's will and trust in His good plans. Remember to lean on Jesus Christ, our Lord and Savior, who willingly and lovingly sacrificed himself for our redemption.

On a final note, if you do not know who Jesus Christ is, I would like to introduce you to Him. Jesus Christ is the son of God sent from heaven to earth to die on the cross for our human sins. He was the spotless, sinless sacrifice used to pardon the world for us to be reconciled with God. "For this is how God loved the world: He gave his one and only Son, so that everyone who believes in him will not perish but have eternal life" (John 3:16). I would highly encourage you to read John 3:16 in whichever Bible translation you best understand and quietly meditate on its meaning. If and when you are ready, please read the prayer below. It is a prayer inviting Jesus Christ into your heart as your Lord and Savior. Obtaining salvation is easy, and it is free to all who wish to receive it.

Dear Jesus: The verse John 14:6 records your words of declaration: "I am the way, the truth, and the life. No one can come to the Father except through me." I believe your words and trust you are my redeemer. I confess I am a sinner and ask for your forgiveness of all my sins. Thank you for your selfless sacrifice on the cross and for dying to save me. I accept you as my Lord and Savior. Fill me with the Holy Spirit and reconcile me with God the Father. Stay with me forever, guiding me each day. **Amen.**

CHAPTER TWENTY-SEVEN

Food for Thought

"Why is life given to those with no future, those God has surrounded with difficulties?"
Job 3:23

From the time we learned to speak and likely till our dying days, we have asked the question, "Why?" We may have wondered, "Why me, why now, and why did this happen?" Strikingly, many have even uttered, "Why is God allowing me to suffer?" I wish I could ease our minds and answer our "why" questions fully and satisfyingly, but the unhappy truth is I cannot. This type of clarity only comes from our Triune God: God the Father, Jesus Christ, and the Holy Spirit.

A PERFECTLY IMPERFECT PREEMIE MOM

For me, it took many years of heartache, prayer, and introspection before I began to feel peace and acceptance with my life as a preemie mom. I spent countless days struggling emotionally and spiritually. At my worst, I felt like Job: "I have no peace, no quietness. I have no rest; only trouble comes" (Job 3:26). Conversely, there were days that were very, very good like when I got to witness my baby's first steps and hear his first words. I felt pride in each growth milestone reached and gratitude for every year that passed. No doubt about it, my life's journey as a preemie mom was tough. I experienced growing pains to a degree I never had before. But what seemed like punishment at the time was, in actuality, a blessing in disguise because God used my suffering to mold me and shape me into a better version of myself. In essence, I became a person who wanted to live her life more in the vein of Jesus Christ.

Life is hard, and contrary to popular belief, I do not believe we were ever promised easy and carefree lives. In fact, the Bible is full of stories of people who had suffered immensely despite maintaining close relationships with God. Well-known examples include Abraham, Jacob, Joseph, Moses, Ruth, Elijah, Esther, David, Peter, John the Baptist, John the Apostle, and the Apostle Paul. Though, it is my humble opinion that Jesus Christ was the greatest sufferer of all time. Isaiah 53:5-6 prophesied the pain that Jesus Christ experienced for all of us: "But he was pierced for our rebellion, crushed for our sins. He was beaten so we could be whole. He was whipped so we could be healed. All of us, like sheep, have strayed away. We have left God's paths to follow our own. Yet the Lord laid on him the sins of us all."

Though Jesus Christ was perfect, He experienced the worst. Through His death on the cross and His resurrection three days later, we were also granted another promise: "I have told you all this so that you may have peace in me. Here on earth you will have many trials and sorrows. But take heart, because I have overcome the world." (John 16:33). Jesus Christ overcame His earthly sufferings, and I firmly believe He can help us do the same.

"Why" questions directed at God always remind me of the Biblical character of Job. I first studied the book of Job in an undergraduate English class focusing on apologetics. For those who have not read the Book of Job, I highly encourage you to do so. Through his story, I learned a lot about human nature and its fallibility before God; most importantly, I got a tiny glimpse of how great God truly is. While I learned that God allows people to suffer (even the innocent ones), I also learned that His sovereignty, power, wonder, and sense of justice are undeniably beyond my ability to fully comprehend. Now, on to Job's story.

Job lived a blameless life before God. He was blessed with a large family and a vast estate, and though he was very wealthy, Job chose to fear God and stay away from evil. The Book of Job goes on to describe a day when the heavenly court convenes. On this day, God speaks to Satan positively about Job. After this, it is recorded, "Satan replied to the Lord, 'Yes, but Job has good reason to fear God. You have always put a wall of protection around him and his home and his property. You have made him prosper in everything he does. Look how rich he is! But reach out and take away everything he has, and he will surely curse you to your face!'" (Job 1:9-11).

So, in His infinite wisdom, God gives Satan permission to test Job, and by the end of the first chapter, we find Job sinless and suffering.

Though Job seemingly lost everything he had all at once, he never blames God. Instead, he proclaims, "I came naked from my mother's womb, and I will be naked when I leave. The Lord gave me what I had, and the Lord has taken it away. Praise the name of the Lord!" (Job 1:21). Despite his tragic and overwhelming circumstances, Job never sins in the first chapter. When I first read this, I was amazed by Job's perseverance and character. Even though he lost his beloved children and earthly possessions, Job continued to honor God during the most difficult time of his life. If only for Job's sake, I wished his story ended here. (Stop while you are ahead, Job!) But instead, his story gets worse. God was not yet finished with Job, and He had a lot more points to make, all of which exist for our benefit.

So, God—in His infinite wisdom—allows Satan to test Job one more time. Now with his whole body covered in terrible boils, Job continues to defend God's honor in front of his wife. But once his friends arrive, Job's anguish gets the better of him. Though he does not curse Him, he begins to question God's judgment. Specifically, Job questions his current path in life, as well as God's reasons for allowing it to happen. His bitter complaining worsens, and in his state of distress, he finally accuses God of unfair mistreatment. In doing this, a once sinless Job is now a sinner.

Despite his nonstop profession of innocence, Job's friends accuse him of committing some sort of past sin because, after all, he must have done something to warrant his current state of "punishment." However, in

108

recalling the beginning of the story, it was not God who was hurting Job—it was Satan. Job's friends were very wrong about God's character, and because of these misconceptions, Job was further led astray spiritually. Instead of believing in their friend or interceding in prayer on his behalf, Job's friends continue to accuse and speak falsities about him and God's nature. Make no mistake, God was watching, and after an especially long-winded chastisement from Job's friend, God steps in to correct them all.

From a whirlwind, God asks Job, "Who is this that questions my wisdom with such ignorant words? Brace yourself like a man, because I have some questions for you, and you must answer them" (Job 38:1-3). Thus begins God's holy response. He asks Job to explain himself, as well as many of God's miraculous wonders of nature. Some of my favorite verses are Job 38:31-33, where God asks, "Can you direct the movement of the stars—binding the cluster of the Pleiades or loosening the cords of Orion? Can you direct the constellations through the seasons or guide the Bear with her cubs across the heavens? Do you know the laws of the universe? Can you use them to regulate the earth?" To me, God's words were poetic and profoundly scientific. His questions were simply divine, and through them, we get tiny glimpses of how powerful, majestic, and precious God truly is.

After His intense speech, God finally asks Job, "Do you still want to argue with the Almighty? You are God's critic, but do you have the answers?" (Job 40:2). Job then proclaims he does not have the answers and is not worthy of saying anything else. It was the right call. If we, as humans, fail to understand the mysteries of the world we live in, how could we expect to understand the things that unfold in the heavens or even the mysteries of God? Simply put, we cannot. Our human capacity to understand these things is sorely limited, and I have learned to be okay with this.

Once my son turned three years old, he began to speak eloquently in whole sentences. I was so happy because his milestones were generally delayed, but thankfully he was now ahead of the curve. The downside to my son's gift of gab was his plethora of new "why" questions, most of which were directed at me. Although I listened intently to his questions, I refrained from answering most since my responses were either not age-appropriate, outside his current developmental ability to grasp, or hard to understand without having had certain life experiences. Often, I would defer my answers to another time and tell him we could revisit the topic when he was much older. Or if I was feeling especially cheeky, I would completely change the subject or distract him with something else in the near vicinity. Does the use of redirection ring a bell? I am reminded of the verse Matthew 7:11 which says, "So if you sinful people know how to give good gifts to your children, how much more will your heavenly Father give good gifts to those who ask him." As a human, my redirection was not always pure of heart, but with God, His redirection of Job was not at all evil and done only out of love. In the end, God restores Job's health, doubles his fortunes, and provides him with a new family once Job sincerely and earnestly repents for his actions.

There are seven important lessons that I take away from the story of Job. First, human suffering does not come from the hands of God; it comes from

Satan. Second, God allows suffering to occur in people (even in the innocent and sinless). Third, praising God in both the good times and the bad is essential in life. Fourth, although God may gently correct us later, He does allow us to ask our "why" questions. Fifth, God gives opportunities for repentance and forgiveness always. Sixth, be judicious in choosing your friends. Seventh, God is sovereign in all situations, and He can restore us at any time He chooses.

The Book of Job foreshadows a very important aspect of Christianity. In chapter nine, Job laments that he is without a mediator to help him approach God for mercy: "God is not a mortal like me, so I cannot argue with him or take him to trial. If only there were a mediator between us, someone who could bring us together. The mediator could make God stop beating me, and I would no longer live in terror of his punishment. Then I could speak to him without fear, but I cannot do that in my own strength" (Job 9:32-35). Job is a clear example of mankind's need for Jesus Christ as an intercessor. Job hit the nail on the head. As humans, we are also mortal before God, but Jesus Christ, God's one and only son, has the power and authority to act as our mediator before God. "There is one God and one Mediator who can reconcile God and humanity—the man Christ Jesus" (1 Timothy 2:5). Through the grace of God, we have access to our mediator every single day.

The Apostle Paul once wrote, "And we know that God causes everything to work together for the good of those who love God and are called according to his purpose for them" (Romans 8:28). That means God can use "bad things" for both our good and His purpose. It can be further surmised that God's allowances of suffering and painful experiences are honorable. In looking back, I believe my preemie baby was a huge blessing for me. He served God's good purpose of removing the destructive things in my life: my love for idols, my need for control, and my belief that God did not care about me. God used my struggles as a preemie mom to restore our relationship. So, do not fear, preemie moms and dads. God will not let your suffering last forever. Like Job, when you reverently seek Him, God will restore you and make your life whole again.

CHAPTER
TWENTY-EIGHT

A Love that Never Fails

"Understand, therefore,
that the Lord your God is indeed God.
He is the faithful God who keeps his covenant
for a thousand generations and lavishes
his unfailing love on those who love him and
obey his commands."
Deuteronomy 7:9

Much time has passed since we first welcomed our son into the world. Our once fragile preemie has flourished into a healthy and happy boy. With his friendly and dynamic personality, he is an absolute joy to be around. Friends and strangers alike often remark they would never have guessed he was born prematurely. God grew him from a delicate NICU baby into the youthful boy he is today. I am so grateful to God for this!

My start to preemie motherhood was full of ups and downs. On my best days, I freely bonded with my son and kept God close in my heart. When things were so-so, I would push down the FOMO and focus on being a doting, loving mom. At my worst, all I could do was tell myself to "breathe, just breathe." God used my time and experiences as a preemie mom to mold me and embolden me for my good and His glory. "And yet, O Lord, you are our Father. We are the clay, and you are the potter. We all are formed by your hand" (Isaiah 64:8).

For those enduring their own preemie-related trials, it is my sincere wish that my testimony serves as a source of encouragement and comfort. God made me, Jesus saved me, and the Spirit inspired me. I am here today as a testament of God's love and powerful healing and to celebrate that God is good and His promises are forever!

A Psalm of a Preemie Mom

Almighty Father,
Breath of life,
Console my heart,
Deliver my baby.
Everlasting God,
Forever unfailing,
Give me peace,
Hear my prayers
In heaven above.
Jesus Christ,
Kindness incarnate,
Loves my child,
Miraculously heals,
Never fails.
O merciful God,
Protector of preemies,
Quiet my heart,
Release me from
Snares abounding.
Take my fears,
Unravel the mysteries.
Victory or defeat,
With my Savior,
Xristos, I survive.
Yahweh, I am
Zealous for you.

A Note from Dawn

It is my absolute pleasure to share with you my preemie story!
If you enjoyed *A Perfectly Imperfect Preemie Mom,*
please consider leaving a book review.

As always, it is my sincerest wish that my memoir of hope and healing
reaches those who need it, while giving God the glory in magnificent ways.

If you would like to connect, please visit me on Instagram
@dawnkimromo

www.ingramcontent.com/pod-product-compliance
Lightning Source LLC
Chambersburg PA
CBHW030316130626
46549CB00002B/887